T0311551

Cash, Corruption and Economic Development

Have you ever asked yourself what gives comfort to someone who demands and accepts a bribe, sells drugs or commits professional crimes for money? The majority of these people are not wealthy, and they accept small amounts of money every day from their victims.

Cash, Corruption and Economic Development examines the causes of corruption and crime and highlights what brings comfort to all those who accept bribes and kickbacks, arguing that it is paper currency because it does not leave a signature of its movement from one entity to another. The author proposes that today, with the technology available, we can make the transition to a paper currency-free economy, which will help reduce corruption and crime and give a boost to economic development. The book analyses the causes of corruption and presents a replacement for the current model, to be implemented by a central bank and followed by banks operating within its jurisdiction.

This book will be of interest to economists, students of economics and finance, and all those who have suffered as a result of corruption and professional crime and want these practices to end.

Vikram Vashisht is a Certified Practising Accountant (CPA), Master of Accounting, Bachelor of Laws (LLB) and Bachelor of Commerce (BCom), and has previously served as a finance officer in the Australian Army.

Routledge Focus on Economics and Finance

The fields of economics are constantly expanding and evolving. This growth presents challenges for readers trying to keep up with the latest important insights. Routledge Focus on Economics and Finance presents short books on the latest big topics, linking in with the most cutting-edge economics research.

Individually, each title in the series provides coverage of a key academic topic, whilst collectively the series forms a comprehensive collection across the whole spectrum of economics.

Cash, Corruption and Economic Development

Vikram Vashisht

LONDON AND NEW YORK

First published 2017
by Routledge
2 Park Square, Milton Park, Abingdon, Oxon OX14 4RN

and by Routledge
605 Third Avenue, New York, NY 10017

First issued in paperback 2021

Routledge is an imprint of the Taylor & Francis Group, an informa business

Publisher's Note
The publisher has gone to great lengths to ensure the quality of this reprint but points out that some imperfections in the original copies may be apparent.

British Library Cataloguing-in-Publication Data
A catalogue record for this book is available from the British Library

Library of Congress Cataloguing-in-Publication Data
A catalog record for this book has been requested

ISBN 13: 978-1-03-209688-9 (pbk)
ISBN 13: 978-1-138-06386-0 (hbk)

Typeset in Times New Roman
by Out of House Publishing

For all of us to live a life of dignity and respect, today and tomorrow, no matter in which part of the world we live, no matter how rich we are, visibility of movement of money from one entity to another, when required to be looked into as determined by the law of the land, is the only solution.

Contents

Illustrations

Figure

Tables

Preface

This book does not discuss how we can time travel, this book does not discuss how human colonies can be set up on the Moon, Mars or beyond, this book does not discuss any concepts of science that could open new doors into dimensions unknown to us so far – but what *is* discussed in this book could be the start of a new era for humankind, for the present generation and for generations to come.

The human race today can be divided into two distinct groups: those who are resourceful and those who are not; those who have enough to eat and those who are hungry; those who have the protection of laws and those who don't; those who sun tan and those who work under 45 degree Celsius heat and still find it hard to afford a meal; those who live like humans and those who don't. But despite this, we live in the best time of human history because conditions were even worse a century ago and the possibility of a better tomorrow – not for a few people but for the whole human race – is more real than ever before.

So, what does this book discuss? This book discusses how it can be made very difficult for the corrupt, the professional criminals and anti-social elements to carry on their activities. It is corruption and crime that deny many of us what we should have as human beings. We all suffer from crime and corruption, some in big ways and some in small, some directly and some indirectly. The menace of corruption has caused immense grief to humanity over the ages. It has slowed our development down and has contributed to wars and suffering. It has denied people the right to food, medicine and equal opportunity. For as long as this menace of corruption exists, we the people who inhabit this planet are not going to live in peace. This book analyses the fundamental factor that provides comfort to the corrupt and the criminals when they are engaging in their antisocial activities. For as long as this menace of corruption exists, we the people who inhabit this planet are not going to live in peace.

So, what is that fundamental factor that provides comfort to the corrupt to engage in corruption? It is the fact that the movement of paper currency from one entity to another does not leave a visible signature or trail of its movement. For example, I give someone 100 dollars – how can I prove that I gave it to him and who is watching? No one is watching; this is the comfort that all the corrupt and criminal have when they indulge in corrupt and criminal activities. If we take this comfort away from them then we can deter them from indulging in antisocial activities, because they do this for money and they will know that their transactions are visible and are not hidden. How can that be done? That can be done by stopping the use of paper currency and by making it mandatory within your jurisdiction that all payments are made electronically when money travels between bank accounts to settle transactions.

We see that every day there are new technological inventions changing and improving our lives, but as far as paper currency is concerned, we are still where we were many decades ago. We need to move forward, we need to advance, we need to take the next step – and that next step, if taken to reduce corruption and crime, will have a huge impact on our society. The invention of paper currency must have given a huge boost to our economies but its very nature is the cause of the professional crime and corruption present within our communities and countries. Perhaps the transition to a paper currency-free economy would have been more like a daydream fifty years back, but it is possible today. It will bring with it all the benefits of paper currency plus the visibility that is possible only when payments are made electronically from one bank account to another.

Selfish as we are, possible it is that some of us may, and quite a few of us do, put our own good before what is just and good for the community, realising not that our stay here on this planet is only temporary. The human mind is clever, it provides a logic for every wrong that we do. So, it is good to have a system which will ensure that there is less room for anyone to commit acts of corruption and crime. This book discusses such a system.

I have not discussed in this book how much corruption is taking place in any particular part of the world or in the world as a whole, or which drugs are sold in which part of the world, or how many people are illegally trafficked every year, or how many people become victims of the illegal human organ trade, or how many women are forced into illegal prostitution, or how many influential people avoid prison because they are influential. That information is available in plenty in the media around us. You only need to type a few words into a search engine on the internet and you will see the extent of corruption in society. What I *have* discussed in this book is how these crimes can be stopped. Millions of people around the globe become victims of crimes that are unimaginable to most of us. The media around us is filled with the occurrences of such crimes: we simply need to take a look and some of us may not be able to sleep that night.

The prime minister of some country once said that out of every 100 units of money spent by the government of that country for the welfare of the common man, only seventeen units reached him. The story of economic development in that country would have been very different had there been no corruption there. It would have taken them only one year to achieve what they took six to do and it might have taken them sixty years to reach where they could have been in ten. If that is the story of one country, then many others may also share the same story and might have shared the same fate.

The transition to a paper currency-free economy could be the start of a world that is free from corruption and certain crimes. It could radically transform our communities into communities where corruption and crime will be very hard to commit. This book suggests a way as to how we can become a society, a community or a country where the corrupt are unable to demand and accept bribes and kickbacks, and where the professional criminals and sellers of contraband are unable to commit their crimes for money and are not able to sell the contraband.

The absence of corruption and crime today or a relatively lower level of crime and corruption in your part of the world does not mean that you are vaccinated against it. A low degree of crime and corruption can move to a high degree if the conditions that ensure a low degree of crime and corruption lose their strength. But the transition to a paper currency-free economy will make it very difficult for the corrupt and criminals to accept bribes or kickbacks or commit crimes for money, which in turn will ensure that your country will remain free from corruption and crime and may enjoy the level of development that it presently does because corruption siphons money meant for development out of the system, and crime hurts the community by making it hard for businesses to flourish because no investor will invest in a country that is infested with corruption and crime. They may and will choose a better destination.

Whether privately owned online currencies are accepted by your banks, allowed to be traded or used to make payments within your jurisdiction is an issue for your government to decide. Their impact on your economy today or in the future is a matter for your government to deliberate. Their impact on the stability of your economy and on the economic development of your country is for your government to think over and decide. Their impact on the volume of money supply within your jurisdiction and consequently on the rate of inflation is for your government to examine. Their impact on the ability of certain entities to move money internationally is for your government to think over and decide, but the logic behind this book is simple: if the movement of money between entities can stay hidden and does not leave a visible trail of who paid whom, who gave money to whom, then the conditions are perfect for corruption, bribery, kickbacks, professional crime and sale of contraband. What should never be allowed is the movement of money from one entity to another and from one account to another that does not leave a visible and identifiable trail. An environment of invisibility surrounding the movement of money is a haven for the corrupt and the criminals, and we will never be able to create corruption-free and crime-free societies unless the movement of money from one entity to another and from one account to another is visible and identifiable.

This book does not discuss how much currency should enter the system electronically, that being a part of the monetary policy of your government. The transition to a paper currency-free economy will be a step towards safer, peaceful and corruption-free communities. Most countries, whether they are developed or developing, can start the process of transition towards a paper currency-free economy.

We are moving towards a time where the use of paper currency will decrease. If paper currency is allowed to settle even a small percentage of transactions in an economy, then the benefits of a paper currency-free economy will not be realised – because use of paper currency for unlawful activities, such as receiving bribes, the sale of contraband or other criminal activities, will still take place. People who intend to indulge in unlawful activities without leaving a visible trail will use paper currency. So, for no corruption and no professional crime to be realised, it is imperative that the use of paper currency is prohibited by law.

The model of settlement of payments discussed in this book explains what will act as legal tender, how payments can be made and settled between banks and how central banks can control the volume of money within their economic jurisdictions after paper currency is recalled and ceases to be legal tender.

It cannot be emphasised enough that the transition to a paper currency-free economy is not about having access to or using internet banking and as such should not be confused with it. Cash sits in the wallets of buyers and in the safes of sellers; in the wallets of buyers it would be replaced by debit cards and in the safes of sellers it would be replaced by electronic payment terminals. That is how simple it is, and that is the easiest and most convenient way to become a paper currency-free economy. Use of mobile phones or the internet for the transfer of money is an option but the bottom line has to be a debit card in the hands of a buyer and an electronic payment terminal in the hands of a seller; these are part of the infrastructure that a government needs to put in place before becoming a paper currency-free economy. Mobile, wireless payment terminals are available today, so a new invention is not needed.

The transition to a paper currency-free economy is not a question of 'IF', but of 'WHEN'. The sooner we do it, the sooner we will create a better world.

1   We the people

We are at the best time in the history of humankind. Look at our history so far – from being barbaric and uncivilised just a few centuries or perhaps a few decades ago, we have transformed ourselves into a more civilised society. Not totally civilised as yet, but the progress made so far compels us to hope that more can be achieved for everyone who lives on this planet. Compare 'us' at the present day to 'us' a century back; the overall situation has changed for the good. More of us have enough to eat and most of us have more legal protection than we had 100 years ago. Things were even worse 200 years back. Laws have improved, the global economy has improved and more of us today are contributing to the global economy as producers and consumers than ever before. Our understanding of the phenomena around us has improved, which has led to the development of technology. Many parts of the world are developed, many are developing and many will start to develop in the near future. But the longer the delay in the development of those underdeveloped parts, the more will be the suffering that people who live in those underdeveloped parts have to go through.

We are at a junction where we can make our civilisation the best in our history. If we keep on developing in a sustainable way and avoid any major wars and conflicts, there is a real chance that some day all of us living in all parts of the world will be able to live a life of prosperity and peace. A very simple example of the peaceful coexistence of different nationalities was the formation of the European Union (EU). If peace and prosperity can be achieved in one part of the world, there is no reason why it cannot be done in any other part of the world. Some extra effort may be needed but there is nothing stopping any country from achieving 100 per cent literacy or creating conditions for businesses to flourish. During the Second World War, many countries in Europe fought against each other. At the end of the war who would have dared to envision an EU as it exists today? The EU today is a reality. What allowed the original member states of the EU to come together was their similar level of economic development, among other factors. Any number of other uniting or common factors may not have helped the formation of the EU had the level of economic development been grossly uneven. A union was formed that allowed people to move and work freely, but that also let the member countries retain their basic character and shape. Just like the EU, a global union is possible for the whole world; it is possible that you could live and work in any part of the world regardless of where you were born, but it is not possible at the moment because the conditions are not right.

As long as slogans of regionalism and narrowness such as 'Antarctica for Antarcticans' are alive and believed, the chances of another war cannot be ruled out. We must know each other very well otherwise we are selfish, myopic and corrupt enough to provoke ourselves to kill and get killed. When you have the ability to go across to the other side of a border and meet the people there, the chances of a war are substantially reduced. This is because it is easier to fight against someone you have never met and harder to fight against someone you know. The formation of the EU was a step towards a world where the impact of political boundaries on travel and work opportunities may become minimal. This leaves us with the question as to why do we need a world where the impact of political boundaries will be minimal? We need it for the betterment of our own civilisation and out of sheer need. Until we are free to travel and see what happens on the other side of the border, there is a chance that the hatred inside the human mind may not go away. There is a chance that you may let someone else feed you his or her thoughts without being able to see the truth. The existence of conditions that will not restrict people from travelling is needed. For peace to be here on this planet, people on all sides of all the fences need to understand the value of peace and a peaceful and prosperous life. But for anyone to value a peaceful life they must have a peaceful life; we cannot understand the value of something we do not have. Peace for a hungry stomach is food; as long as someone is hungry, he or she cannot be at peace.

Underdevelopment of many parts of the world poses a threat to our own civilisation. Prosperity and education need to hit every part of the world for every one of us to live in peace. Development of the whole world is the requirement for peace to exist here, forever. It is imperative that people living in each and every country start enjoying economic prosperity and a peaceful life. People who cannot make ends meet resort to fighting. So long as your neighbour is hungry and uneducated, you are not secure inside your house. And in this age of fast travel, 'neighbourhood' will have to be defined very liberally. Just being fed is not enough – being educated is equally important as education teaches us everything, including the value of peace and freedom. Until that is achieved, our civilisation is not great. Peace is, wherever it has been and wherever it will be, a product of economic prosperity and education.

If the people from underdeveloped parts of the world who would be willing to migrate to developed parts of the world were allowed to move, the economies of the developed countries would collapse, being unable to bear the additional load of migrants. The economic development of the whole world is needed, especially of the underdeveloped parts of it, to reduce the chances of war and to increase the chances of peace. Imagine you had the ability to settle down in any part of the world and enjoy the same conditions that you enjoy today. Imagine this for any other human being who is living in any other part of the world. Many countries that are at peace with each other were not so some time back. What has changed and why are they not fighting? It is because they are prosperous and they appreciate the importance of peace. Will you fight against a country or let your government wage a war against a country where you could go and live a free, prosperous and peaceful life? Until every citizen of the world is prosperous and at peace, the threat of terrorism and war will loom over our heads. But political boundaries are very much needed. They will always be needed as much as they are needed today. Without political boundaries and governments responsible for governance within their political boundaries, the world would be chaotic. Of course, we do not want chaos. Political boundaries are needed just the way they are; it is their impact on us that should be minimal and which will bring immense hope for each of us. The free movement of people across the borders and reduced impact of political boundaries will be the result of economic prosperity for the whole human race.

If all the people living within the EU can travel and work within the EU, why can the people living in other parts of the world not travel to any other part of the world and work there? Who stops them, and why? At least at present it is not possible because of the wide income disparities that exist between different countries. Only the economic development of all countries can minimise the impact of political boundaries. The economic conditions in many parts of the world will need to be improved. The prevalence of uneven economic conditions is not letting people travel across the borders. For example, Australia and New Zealand are two different countries with two distinct governments and systems. But it is not that difficult for an Australian to work and settle down in New Zealand, and the same is true in reverse. This is possible because the level of economic development in both the countries is the same. Certainly, both countries share many other values, but without the same level of economic development, this level of freedom of movement for the residents of these two countries would not have been possible.

So, what is stopping the underdeveloped countries from developing? What is the major factor that is preventing billions from getting above the poverty line? What is not letting hundreds of millions receive an education? What is not letting this happen fast? Why do some countries develop fast and some not? A simple one-word answer is 'corruption', the corruption that exists in many countries. How can corruption be the root cause of all evil? Just a simple example: when money that is allocated by the government of a country to developmental projects ends up in the pockets of unintended corrupt recipients, development is set back. This money, if spent on its intended purpose, would have helped develop that part of the world. This money, if spent as planned, would have created conditions and jobs for people to earn a living. Corruption in countries where it is rampant is not just a one-off occurrence; it happens on a daily basis. So, every time corruption happens, development gets a setback. Moreover, the low and slow rate of development brings pain to billions and keeps the chances of war and terrorism alive. The sufferers in any war or an incident of terrorism are never the countries. The sufferers are the people. It is the people who feel the pain.

Sustainable economic development of the whole world, touching each and every human being, is the solution for global peace – for all men and women to stay with their families in happiness and not be sent to war. Look at any war, either recent or not so recent – did it create better economic conditions for the masses? Human lives are lost in every war; the side that loses least claims victory. Would you really call it a victory? The world will become a much safer place when we realise that this entire planet of ours, and not just the land marked by a political boundary, is our motherland. How could only the area under the control of a particular government be my motherland and not the rest? Either the whole planet is my motherland or no part of it.

The special attachment that we have towards our race, country or religion, and which makes some of us act irrationally at times, is not going to go away until all of us know all of us very well and until all of us become prosperous and educated. This is possible only through economic development, and for economic development it is mandatory that there is no corruption, and that the money is spent on its intended purpose and does not end up in the pockets of the corrupt. And to see whether money has been spent on its intended purpose, it is imperative that the flow of money from one entity to another is visible.

A developed world is in the interest of everyone. It is possible to think of it today and it can be a reality. Perhaps the idea of a prosperous and educated world would have been unimaginable a few centuries ago, but so would the technology and development of today. Today our efforts could make development happen in all parts of the world. The sooner it happens the better it is for us. We are the people who become part of governments, be it a democratic government or non-democratic one. And as responsible citizens we must understand that expansion of the empire is not going to do any good to our people but consolidation will. The days when governments of countries used to expand their empires are over. You can feel proud that your country has a very big and strong military but as an enlightened citizen you must ask yourself what that big and strong military is getting you. Feeling good and proud of the military strength of your country is one thing but what in real terms is this military strength getting you? This is a question that we should ask ourselves: is a powerful army ensuring social security, creating better living conditions, reducing the level of crime in the community, ensuring that medical care is available when it is needed, or schooling your children to help them live better lives? The more strongly you ask these questions, the higher is the chance of more economic development. As an enlightened citizen, you must ask your government if the money is spent on national defence or on the ability to project power. The same money that is spent on the projection of military power could have been spent on health care, education or infrastructure development, adding value to the lives of the citizens of your country. The same money spent on health care would have saved lives.

Coming back to the first point, if people who become part of a government are enlightened, they can frame government policies that are good for the masses. Countries that are experiencing strong economic growth and emerging as economic powers must not try to expand their empires. They must rather try to consolidate this opportunity to strengthen their countries. Regardless of anything it is the truth that wins in the end. They should not let go easily of this opportunity, which they have received after hundreds of years. A simple look at recent and not so recent history shows us that countries and empires that could have made the lives of their citizens better did not do so and instead were more eager to establish their hegemony over others. That strategy has never worked in human history and it will not work in the future. It is more the responsibility of the people who form policies to see this. It is for the leaders of countries to see that making their citizens educated and prosperous will make their countries immensely strong internally, forever, whereas spending money on military power at the cost of internal development may just make them strong on the outside and hollow inside. Uplifting their citizens by educating them and removing any obstacles in the path of their economic development will make their countries truly strong. If that is achieved, even with decent military strength, your country will be much stronger than having a huge military and hollowness inside. It is imperative that we think of what wins in the long run. An educated and economically strong civilisation that knows how to stay economically strong and understands the value of education will always be strong and prosperous. The sooner we abandon the myopic vision the better it is for us. What threat is there that was not there before and must be given deep thought before more money is spent on military build-up? If there is no new threat and more money is poured into the military, then it is towards power projection and not defence.

If a country has historically been a more significant military power than you and has never attacked you, why will it attack you now when you are economically much stronger? Strengthening your countries on the inside by making your populace educated and economically prosperous will make them able to withstand anything. Think about making your country immortal and not just a short-lived actor in human history. That can be achieved only if the citizens of your country are educated and economically prosperous. What is important is that we do not let this opportunity slip by. We should not let ourselves fall back to the Stone Age. It was a 'Stone Age' on this planet when during the Second World War we showed no respect for human lives in any part of the world. Just imagine a soldier on any side – did he have any power to change anything? Probably not; well, let's remove any doubts here, definitely not. So, who has the responsibility to change the course of things and contribute, to make a change to the path that our own civilisation takes for betterment? It is the men and women who are enlightened and are in a position of authority and leadership. It is the men and women who are enlightened and who can influence those who are in a position of authority and leadership.

Now to the money side of the house. An argument can be that the money spent by a government within an economy helps the economy flourish and lets the economic cycle move. Let's take this example: a government has 100 dollars and it spends those 100 dollars on its military.

It could have spent this money on many other activities as discussed above but it did not. By spending 100 dollars on its military, it immediately lost 100 dollars that it could have spent on educating its citizens or on providing medical care and saving the lives of its citizens or on hundreds of other developmental activities. The options are simple: a government can either make a bomb or it can build infrastructure and spend money on development. Once a resource is spent, it is spent. Explaining further, those 100 dollars spent on non-military activities internally would have generated at least the same economic activity as those spent on military activity, but the government would have had 100 dollars more for developmental activities such as education, medical care, infrastructure development etc. Secondly, when a road, hospital, school or train network is developed, the community gets the benefit for many years to come compared to money spent on the acquisition of military hardware, although the equivalent money is spent on both of them.

Corruption is a major cause of development being slower than what its actual speed can be. In countries where corruption exists, and the list is very long, many people embezzle public funds allocated for development. A very small number of pockets absorb a substantial percentage of the money allocated for development, leading to setbacks in development. Let's say that funds were allocated to build an electricity generation plant but the plant was never built because corrupt officials embezzled all the funds. Had the plant been built, the power generated would have run factories, which would have provided employment to people living in that region, which would have created economic prosperity, which would have created peace in that region, which would have created additional tax revenue for the government to spend on developmental activities. A casual look around will make anyone aware as to the level of corruption that exists in this world. The level of corruption that some people get involved in defies all principles of mathematics or logic. They are causing a lot of pain and grief to billions.

Working for a reward is in our very nature as human beings. Any system that creates conditions for people who want to work hard to excel is bound to prosper. A system that does not reward hard-working people will not flourish as much. It is imperative that conditions are created which allow people who work hard to reap the benefits of their hard work. This will allow any society to progress further and become prosperous. Compare this to a system where everyone gets paid the same wage. Will anyone put in any extra effort? Why should they? There is no incentive for them. Conditions certainly need to be created that allow people to realise their full potential. If the conditions are not right, enterprise in any society is not possible. The incentives for hard work have to be there. The primary condition is preferably no crime rate or a very low crime rate. Again, to achieve a low crime rate, people living within a community should have employment and education. A full stomach enjoys peace but may not understand the value of peace. It is a full stomach and an educated mind that fully understand the value of peace. So, people living within a society need employment and education for the right conditions to exist for enterprise. When tax revenue is spent on education, job creation and other social welfare activities, the impact of that on the whole society is that conditions are created for the enhancement of enterprise.

We invented money; we probably would not have needed to, had we not developed our civilisation or chosen to live the way we used to. But now we are here in a society where money buys us what we need. The more we have of it, the more likely it is that we will live satisfactorily. This power of money makes all of us want more of it. More money equals more satisfaction which equals more happiness. This equation will pass most tests. This is what we have seen since the time we were born and if we believe in it, it is very natural. Human effort determines everything and is the sole factor behind economic development – otherwise resources will just be sitting idle. Without human effort, economic development is not possible. Human effort and actions generate wealth or money or any other name you might want to give it. Resources might be present on this beautiful Earth but to create wealth you need to put in the effort. Look at this example: there is a tree loaded with apples. Anyone can pick apples from this tree. Access to this tree is not restricted. Someone raises a fence around that tree and claims that only he has the right to the apples on that tree. This person has just created some wealth for himself. Raising a fence is an effort. Now let's consider another example, where someone did not put in the effort of raising a fence. This guy just verbally told others that this tree with apples was his tree. Still he has put in some effort and created wealth for himself. The factor of demand for apples of course cannot be ignored. Apples are a factor that cause wealth because there is a demand for apples. Had there been no demand for apples, apples in this man's possession would not have generated any wealth for him.

Generating wealth, as much as anyone wants to, within the boundaries of the law is absolutely legitimate. What is not legitimate is corruption, which exists in many countries around the world and poses a serious threat to our very own civilisation. Corruption does not pose a threat only to the countries where it exists but to humanity as a whole. Just as the burning of fossil fuels in one part of the world can contribute to climate change, in the same way, corruption in any part of the world can be the cause of disruption of activities in other parts of the world. Coming back to why and how corruption poses a threat, a simple answer is that when people in one part of the world are hungry, under-developed, malnourished and uneducated, some of them will be eas-ily influenced. They may do anything for money. They probably never experienced peace or prosperity, so if they do not value peace or pros-perity it may not be their fault. This very fact of our nature threatens us. It is not just for this reason that corruption is bad. It is bad because it is simply bad: regardless of how corruption in one part of the world can impact people in any other part of the world, corruption is bad. People who are living in societies where there is corruption have a right to live in a corruption-free world.

Corruption creates scary societies. Imagine a smuggler smuggling human organs without any fear because he bribed all those whose job is to stop him and bring him to justice, or a professional criminal who kid-naps women and children for the purposes of sexual slavery and forces them into prostitution without any fear. Imagine this smuggler's ability to bribe police to register a false complaint against you because you raised your voice against him, or imagine someone testifying against you in exchange for a bribe, or imagine a doctor in a public hospital asking for a bribe before he touches your wounds, or imagine a judge deciding a case against you because he accepted some hard cash from your opponent and that hard cash was the only merit that this judge considered while deciding that case, or imagine a minister of a govern-ment accepting a bribe to award a tender to an entity to build a hospital, or imagine government employees accepting bribes for appointing new employees. The list is endless. The full list is known only to those who make others suffer because of their corrupt practices. Would you want to live in such places? The impact of corruption is a crippled society. A society that suffers from the menace of corruption will never be able to realise its full potential. The sufferers are billions of innocent human beings who suffer the pain but have committed no crime. It can be very easy to sit at home or do your 9–5 job or shift work without knowing much about what is happening around you and feel that it is all good – but it may not be all good and a lot of people might be suffering and no one would know that they are suffering. It is only them or the ones who want to know more about them who know their actual plight.

It can very pertinently be questioned how a reduction in corrup-tion will increase the literacy rate or level of education in a country. Corruption wherever it is rampant is not a one-off occurrence and will not be confined to a particular department. It will be present in every department. If money that is earmarked for educational purposes is spent on its intended purpose and does not end up in the pockets of corrupt officials, the results will be quicker. For example, if a government had allocated resources to build two schools and only one school was built and the money for the other one was embezzled by corrupt officials, then only half the objectives will be achieved. If all the money is spent as planned, the results will be much quicker; literacy rates will increase quickly and people living in that region will get educated quickly. This applies to every activity undertaken by a government.

The creation of money and spending of money are two distinct processes. While money is created out of human effort, its spending determines the development of a society. The more efficient and proportionately wholesome the spending is, the quicker the development will be. Let's take an example: a resource a government has can either be spent on buying bread and feeding its populace with that bread or on teaching its citizens to grow wheat and make bread. Of course, a lot of infrastructure will be required for the second option but the second option is preferable in the long run, as you cannot always be a consumer without producing anything. But why worry about producing wheat when someone else is doing that and we live in a world where trade is possible? This government can exploit its competitive advantage and that of its citizens and produce something that the bread makers want. If everyone is making bread, there will be no trade. If someone is making bread and someone else is making jam, trade is possible and both of them will enjoy a better taste. In all countries, governments spend money on development. Countries where public money has been spent efficiently on its intended purpose have developed faster than countries where public funds landed in the pockets of the corrupt.

Impact of corruption on development

When money is embezzled by the employees of a government for their personal benefit, development suffers and the world suffers. In many countries around the world, corruption is a part of daily life. Governments allocate a part of their tax revenue for developmental purposes. Some of their corrupt officials, whose job is to carry out the apportioning of these funds, embezzle the money instead and/or receive kickbacks. And corrupt officials have a network. They never work in isolation. It can never be that there is just one corrupt official embezzling public funds, there will always be a chain. One corrupt official can never operate by himself or herself; there will always be other people within that network. Generally, it will be the corrupt officials and their superiors and their superior's superiors and so on. So, by the time the money that is allocated from the top reaches the bottom, a percentage or probably all of it will have gone into the pockets of corrupt officials. When bribes are accepted from the employees at the lower end of the chain, a portion of the monies goes right up to the top. All this money that is lost would have been a source of more development, when spent on hospitals it would have saved human lives, when spent on infrastructure it would have created jobs, when spent on the education it would have helped people grow intellectually, understand things better, find jobs, earn a livelihood and understand the value of peace and prosperity. Now because all or some of the governmental allocation for development is lost to corruption, it will have an impact on developmental activities and the sufferer in this case is the human race. All corrupt officials, wherever they are must understand that the public funds they have embezzled could have saved and improved human lives.

Let's take another example. A farmer wants to set up a food processing factory. Because he lives in a corruption-ridden country, he has to bribe government officials to buy the land, to get a loan for his factory, to get approval for its design, to continue construction of the factory and probably at every stage and for everything that can be imagined. Corrupt government officials will demand bribes for anything if they can. Let's assume that in the first instance this farmer has got no money to bribe the government officials. He will not become a producer or a consumer and he will not be able to provide employment to people. The impact of this is that the gross domestic production of the world, which could have gone upwards, stays the same. The employment this farmer could have generated does not happen. The sufferer is the human race. Let's assume that this farmer decides to bribe the government officials. His stock of money is limited. If he could install two machines before, now he may only be able to install one. This will result in reduced production. When an entity has a resource that is limited and has to sacrifice a part of that resource for a non-value-adding activity, then that entity is left with reduced resources to spend on value-adding activities.

A government collects taxes, makes policies and allocates money for various projects and activities. Let's say that the project is to build a better irrigation system and some corrupt officials of the government, who think they cannot be caught, spend only a percentage of the allocated funds on this project and embezzle the rest of the money. Now, had that money been spent on its intended purpose, it would have developed that region and increased the production of agricultural produce. This increase in agricultural produce would have helped humanity in at least two ways: firstly, it would have erased the pain that arises from hunger; secondly, it would have given purchasing power to more of us, which would have increased the demand for goods. Increase in demand for goods would have resulted in more production, which would have increased employment opportunities, which would have given peace and prosperity to more people.

How can we rid ourselves of this ugly and evil menace of corruption? How can some changes to the current system, where currency notes facilitate commerce, end corruption?

Impact of movement of dirty money on development

The movement of 'dirty' money internationally is causing a lot of pain to billions who live in abject poverty. Some politicians and corrupt officials accept kickbacks into their bank accounts far away from the boundaries of their own countries and sell their national wealth for a few numbers that sit in their foreign bank accounts. That money could very well have developed their own countries but now it just sits as a figure somewhere, doing no good to anyone. Their country's national wealth has gone down the drain without doing any good to anyone. The result has been the underdevelopment of those countries where many people live in abject poverty and produce nothing because neither human nor infrastructural development took place. Some meagre donations and charitable funds go to those people but their plight remains the same. That is because they are not provided with the means to engage in production. When they have nothing to produce they have nothing to sell, and when they have nothing to sell they have no money to buy what we the people who produce things can sell to them. The result is unemployment and a struggle to register a good growth rate. Once they start producing they will be able to consume more, which will increase the overall production of the world.

We have witnessed economic crises faced by many countries in many parts of the developed world in the last few years. Economies around the globe struggle to register the required growth because there are no consumers for what we can produce. Some countries are still struggling to totally come out of recession, with clouds of uncertainty casting their shadows over what the future might bring. In addition to other measures that might be required, one measure is to increase the production of goods that you could sell.

People who cannot afford to buy what you produce, can become consumers of your products and services, once they have money in their pockets, which they will have only when they start producing something. These very people who are not producing anything today can engage in production, become consumers and thus fuel the engine for global economic growth. Their economic development will ensure the economic development of other parts of the world. The developed countries that struggle to reach the required economic growth can register more growth if people who are not engaged in production become producers and thereby become consumers. Development needs to take place in every part of the world. People living there are human beings like us. They need what you and I need. They feel the same hunger and pain that we do when we are hungry. Those very people can become the engine for global economic growth, but for that to happen their resources should be used for their human and infrastructural development, right where they live, and should not just sit as a figure in some bank account in a secrecy jurisdiction. Development of the whole world is not an option – we need it for us. Development in developing countries will be faster if they transition to paper currency-free economies.

All efforts to monitor and stop the flow of dirty money should be applauded but at the same time it is imperative that dirty money is not allowed to be created in the first place. That is possible only when you set your house in order. That is possible when those who have dirty money are not able to buy or threaten witnesses and prosecutors by hiring professional criminals and are not able to buy or threaten those whose job it is to bring them to justice. With paper currency present in your economy, you are making their jobs easier because hiring a professional criminal, buying a witness, buying someone to destroy the evidence or buying justice only becomes easy when the movement of paper currency between entities remains invisible. This factor gives the required comfort to all the corrupt and the criminal. This group at the top that accepts kickbacks and bribes would find it very difficult to buy or threaten those who can bring them to justice if each and every transfer of money from one entity to another and from one account to another was visible in the absence of paper currency. So, to have your house in order you need to transition to a paper currency-free economy. It is a big fight in which all of us are involved and all of us are stakeholders. Knowingly or unknowingly, it impacts us all. Tens of trillions of dollars over the past few decades have left our shores and ended up in secrecy jurisdictions.

Factors impacting the level of corruption

The foremost factor that contributes to the level of corruption in any society is the level of self-esteem of the people who live in it; if the level of self-esteem is high then people will not lower themselves to a level where they demand a bribe for a lawful job that they are supposed to

do and for which they are paid a salary, or accept a bribe for an unlawful job that will be detrimental to their community. Such people have
no self-esteem and it is that low level of self-esteem that contributes
to the menace of corruption and crime in a big way. The self-esteem
of an individual is eroded over a period of time; people are not born
with a low level of self-esteem. It starts to be eroded inside homes when
parents adopt an irrational approach towards their children, then at
schools when teachers adopt an irrational approach towards students
and then in the wider community, where we all struggle to prove our
existence to ourselves and in the process destroy the self-esteem of many
around us. But the starting point is at home and school, where you were
not respected in the way you thought you should have been; that level is
relative to what you thought you deserved, but a certain level of behaviour on the part of parents and teachers can be viewed as standard. So,
slowly the erosion of self-esteem starts and eventually it leads to the
corrupt and the criminals present in the society because the self-esteem
they had has been destroyed over time by the irrational behaviour of
people present in their homes, schools and the wider community. And
now they do not care about what you think of them – they simply do
not care whether you call them corrupt or criminals or anything else.

Where the level of education is high, people are more aware of their
rights than in countries where the level of education is low. Level of
education must not be confused with the rate of literacy; the rate of
literacy can be measured whereas the level of education is a bit less
tangible. Many countries in the world, primarily the less developed
ones, are trying to increase their literacy rates and have more people
going to schools and universities, but still corruption remains extant
and rampant. This may primarily be for the reason that the education
system is driven by a focus on literacy. A move to make a child literate
can be a first move towards educating that child, but a mere ability to
recognise letters and numbers is not the end. Level of education will
depend on the system of education that teaches our children the value
of ethics, morality, mutual respect, social behaviour, social responsibility, legal rights and duties. If you teach someone what his rights are,
he is going to remind everyone else of what their duties are. Education
should also teach a child how to become a responsible global citizen.

The impact of the lines drawn as borders may be gone in the next
few centuries, or sooner provided we do not destroy the factors that
ensure our survival. Today our activities impact on each other more
than ever before. For sustainable development and global peace, we
need to teach young children how to become responsible citizens at
the national and international level. Until peace has been achieved

for each and every one of us, it has not been achieved. In a country where people are educated and understand and value their responsibilities as members of the society, the level of corruption is less than in those where people are uneducated and do not understand their responsibilities.

How much people have to struggle to make ends meet determines the level of corruption in a society. When people are educated and able to make ends meet, the likelihood of them indulging in corrupt practices is comparatively less compared to a country where people are uneducated and live in poverty. If you are educated and can look after yourself and your family without indulging in any corrupt practices then you may not indulge in any corrupt practices. Permanent prosperity does not come from outside, it comes from within. Efforts have to be made within a society to make it prosperous. And what causes prosperity? Economic development causes prosperity.

How can economic development occur? What are the factors that cause economic development?

Certainly, there is not just one factor – a whole heap of intertwined factors are responsible for economic development. The ability of an enterprise to flourish within an economy is a very important factor. Societies where it is easy for entities to start production will develop quickly compared to others. Let's take a simple example: 1,000 people live somewhere where their government does not let them do any agriculture. If their government lets them do agriculture, there will be prosperity for them as they will have more to eat. Now let's say that their government allows one entity to perform agriculture and bars everyone else. The government of that country, by doing that, is not letting the rest of the people realise their full economic potential. Now let's say that that government allows all entities to do agriculture but entities have to apply for permissions, permits, licences etc. The start of production in this case is getting delayed by the number of days it takes to get permits and licences. The end result is that economic development is being delayed by the number of days it takes to get the permits and licences. A number of other factors can also be responsible for economic development. For example, the ability of an entity to borrow money to start production may determine whether it starts production. Lenders will lend money quickly when there is an effective mechanism for them to recover their money in the case of a default. Entities find it easier to establish their operations and operate in societies where there is peace. The speed with which the courts of law rule on the economic and business disputes and free the capital in dispute is another very important factor. This discussion shows that there are a number of factors responsible for economic development. The number of factors cannot be restricted and all factors cannot be defined. The actual number may run into thousands. But without production there cannot be economic development and without economic development there cannot be prosperity.

Let's take another example: there is an entity that owns an apple tree and another entity that owns a mango tree. They trade with each other. Now someone else has a tree of bananas; the production of that economy has increased by the value of the bananas produced annually. Had the bananas not been produced, the economic production would not have included the bananas. By allowing the entities within its jurisdiction to grow bananas, or simply by not stopping them from growing bananas, and also by not imposing any barriers to entry on any section of the society on any grounds (denial of entry into the workforce converts a section into pure consumers at a time when that section could very well have become a producer and thereby increased production and subsequently tax revenue), the government allowed economic development within its jurisdiction. It also had more tax revenue because a third entity that was producing bananas started paying taxes (assuming they were running a profitable business). The same tax revenue now could be spent on developmental activities such as education, medical care, infrastructure development and other social welfare activities. The list is endless. This government needs to borrow less because of an increase in its domestic production and a subsequent increase in tax revenue, without increasing the burden of tax on tax-paying entities. The production of bananas should certainly have been stopped had it caused social or environmental damage after utilising the technology currently available. But as it is not causing any environmental or social damage, and the waste is disposed of in an environmentally friendly manner, the production of bananas should be allowed to go ahead.

Level of prosperity and ease of living depend on per capita consumption of goods and services, and the availability of infrastructure per capita. The words 'per capita' have to be paid special attention here because when the number of people sharing infrastructure or production increases without a corresponding increase in infrastructure or production, the level of prosperity and ease of living will decline.

For example, if there are ten buses and 10,000 people living somewhere, then there is one bus for every 1,000 people. Now let's say that the population has gone up to 100,000, then there is one bus for every 10,000 people. The per capita availability of infrastructure in this category has reduced, and people living there will either have to wait longer for a bus journey or the quality of travel by bus will diminish significantly for them.

To maintain a level of prosperity and ease of living, production and population need to find a balance. If growth in production and infrastructure is faster than population growth then prosperity and ease of living will increase, and if population increases faster than production and infrastructure growth then there will be a decline in prosperity and ease of living.

The countries that are towards the bottom of the ladder as far as prosperity and infrastructure development are concerned have to start looking towards increasing their per capita production and consumption and per capita availability of infrastructure. If the increase in production and infrastructure is less than the increase in population, then the level of prosperity will not go up. But to become prosperous fast and to let your populace enjoy a decent quality of life, the growth in production, consumption and infrastructure must be substantially fast, otherwise it will take a lot longer and your populace will have to live without prosperity for a long time. Let's look at the following equations:

1. Your gross domestic product/Your population = Your per capita domestic production
2. Infrastructure available in your country in each category/Your population = Infrastructure available per capita in your country in that category

Compare your per capita production and per capita infrastructure in each and every category with the equivalent in the most developed country in the world.

Now look at where your gross domestic product (GDP) and level of infrastructure development will be in the next five, ten and 20 years.

Next look at if you start controlling your population but can still maintain the same level of production, then what will be the per capita production and per capita availability of infrastructure in X number of years? Also, look at what your GDP and population should be to come to the level of the most developed country in the world. The point here is to control population but still maintain the same level of economic growth so that people who live within your borders can enjoy a better life by having access to more production and more infrastructure.

A huge population cannot be an asset for any country at a time when borders between countries limit the land and resources available, and machines and computers can increase our productivity and the level of ambition in many people stays the same, whether they are twenty-five or fifty.

A very important factor that determines the economic development of a country is the natural resources available to it, which are not infinite you are competing and will have to compete against other countries for them. The availability of the natural resources has and will have an impact on the level of prosperity and ease of living of your populace. And no matter what we may think we can do, one resource, any significant quantity of which we cannot grow, is land – and the more our numbers are, the less is the land available to us per capita. The more our numbers are, the less land we have for agriculture, the less land we have for forests, the less land we have for houses and cities, the less land we have for schools, playgrounds and parks, the less land we have for everything that we do. If you do not want to limit a person's right to the number of children he or she can have during their lifetime, you can control the speed with which they reproduce, so that both you and the new arrivals have access to enough resources and sufficient infrastructure to live a decent life.

We cannot keep on increasing our population without looking at what level this planet can sustain.

The fourth factor that influences the level of corruption in a country is the system of governance. A prosperous and educated society will eventually create an effective system of governance. An inefficient, corrupt system of governance cannot exist in an educated society. People who are aware will demand and make the changes happen. The effectiveness of a system of governance determines the level of honesty of its officials. The procedures and policies followed in a country determine the extent to which corruption can grow. If the officials of the state or another entity feel that there is not a system to audit their activities or they will not be caught when they indulge in corrupt practices, the chances are that in such a society corruption will grow. The presence of a comprehensive, effective, transparent and auditable governance mechanism ensures that corruption in any society is kept under control. The presence of a strong governance mechanism is the key to a corruption-free society.

High levels of education and prosperity support a society becoming corruption free, whereas the presence of a strong governance mechanism ensures that corruption is controlled and not allowed to grow.

The fifth factor that influences the level of corruption is the speed with which the corrupt are brought to justice by the courts of law. Whether people obey the laws of the land depends on their enforcement, and enforcement is not there if the courts of law do not deliver their verdicts fast. When the corrupt and criminal see that the delivery of justice takes decades, it enhances their morale and their fear of the law disappears. When they see that justice is delivered quickly, they will start fearing the law and hesitate before committing any crime. The speed with which the courts of law decide the cases may very well be determined by the number of judges. If one judge decides one case a day, then two judges should decide two cases a day. This formula should apply to a majority of cases. Of course, there will be cases with exceptional backgrounds but for the majority of cases this formula should work. The point under discussion here is that to deliver justice quickly, the number of judges may need to be increased; an increase in the number of judges means that more cases will be attended to by the judges, which implies that they will be able to deliver justice on more cases.

Speedy decisions by courts of law on economic and business disputes also have a positive impact on economic growth. The slow resolution of an economic or business dispute will slow economic development down, while the quick resolution of such disputes will pave the way for faster development. When two or more entities are involved in a dispute over a resource, the development and utilisation of that resource for the time the dispute continues may suffer, as no entity may be able to use it or invest in it. This will slow the economic development down. The resolution of a dispute allows the entity that has established its right over the resource to use it and invest in it. The use of and investment in a resource will increase economic activity, which will help a society develop.

Speed of delivery of justice is required to create fear in the minds of the corrupt and the criminal, but another very important aspect related to this is that people will have a higher regard for the law when they know that speedy justice will be delivered. No society can become civilised without speedy justice. No matter how economically prosperous a society may become, if it is not civilised, it is not worth living there. As discussed above, the speed of justice for most cases depends on the number of judges available, but an increase in the number of judges to impart justice should not be dependent on a politician coming out of his slumber and deciding that the community needs speedy justice. It has to be an ongoing process. The first step is to reckon the maximum time within which a case present before a judge must be decided. Different types of cases may have different time limits; for example a case involving an attempt to murder someone cannot be equated with the recovery of fifty dollars, although both deserve justice. So once the maximum time during which a case must be decided has been set, the next step is to calculate the number of judges required to achieve that target. This will be a very simple arithmetic calculation. The process of monitoring the time taken by a case and the new judges that need to be appointed to keep the time below the limit must be completed by a body that exists specifically for that purpose. It should keep monitoring the time a judge takes to decide a case and appoint new judges accordingly, without any interference from anyone, as long as it is working in accordance with the rules that govern it. It must be understood that the shorter the time frame to decide a case, the more will be the regard for the law in the hearts of the people, and the more will be the fear of the law in the minds of the corrupt and the criminal.

But expansion without supervision will cause chaos. Entities that feel or know that they are not supervised will become corrupt over time, and the quality of their work will decline. Effective performance will require adequate supervision by superiors whose full-time job is supervision. Supervision can be a part-time job of a supervisor where they have other tasks to perform. In that case a supervisor will not give their full attention to supervision. The quality of supervision determines the effectiveness and efficiency of the work performed by subordinates. As such, supervisors must be dedicated supervisors whose sole task is the supervision of other personnel.

An important point regarding decision making. Say you need to go from A to B and there are two roads; using one road the journey will take nine days and using the other it will take eleven days. You have to decide which road to take; the condition here is that you can start your journey only at 7am on any day – if you miss the 7am mark you cannot start at 7.01am and you have to wait for 7am the next day. In this situation, you do not have more than twenty-four hours to decide to save one day because the longer path takes eleven days, which is two days more than the other one. So, if you take one day to decide and follow the path that takes nine days, it will bring the time to ten days. If you take two days to decide and follow the path that takes nine days it will bring the time to eleven days, so you have not saved any time. It would have been better had you started your journey on the path that takes eleven days; in that case, you would have at least familiarised yourself with the route. The point here is that it is possible to argue for twenty days or more over which road to take, but the longest route would have taken only eleven days had a consensus been reached.

Anything that is the job of a government should be a perpetual process which should happen on its own. It should not ordinarily require the leadership to push the government machinery. Leadership cannot fix each and every complaint presented to it one by one; it cannot have the time for that. The job of leadership is to put the hard and soft infrastructure and processes in place that should work on their own without the need for any further prompting. Interference from leadership should come only when the mechanisms in place are not performing as expected; the mechanisms in place should be capable of dealing with the issues and resolving them. Leadership's job is to ensure that the mechanisms are working efficiently and effectively, and to implement ways to improve the efficiency and effectiveness of those mechanisms. At the same time, it looks for newer areas where new mechanisms are needed for the betterment of the community and the country, and puts those mechanisms in place.

The sixth factor that influences corruption and crime is the ability of the institutions of the state to stay insulated from internal and external influences, be they political, monetary or any other. When politicians or powerful people are able to influence the institutions of the state, the whole system becomes nothing but a joke. A majority of the people will obey the rules; it is only a small minority that will try to find ways to break them. When this small minority has the ability to get away with committing a crime by exerting unlawful influence over the institutions of the state, the entire law-enforcing system is nothing but a sham. All the institutions of the state should have the required layers and mechanisms in place to insulate themselves from any undue influences from any quarter.

The seventh factor that determines the level of corruption is the ability of money to remain hidden when moving between entities. Because money is visible the transactions remain invisible. The day money becomes invisible, the transactions will become visible. The ability of money to leave no visible trail when changing hands is a cause of corruption. This factor is very important when corrupt government officials demand bribes, embezzle public funds or accept kickbacks. They know that catching them will be very difficult because the transfer of paper currency from one entity to another leaves no visible trail. For example, if I give you a $50 note, how can I prove that I gave it to you? And who saw it? Where have you kept it? Did I really give it to you? It is hard to prove that.

This book is about how corruption can be stopped. The current banking infrastructure present in many countries should be able to support the transition to a paper currency-free economy.

Corruption is more prevalent in the less developed countries of the world, and the reasons mentioned above help explain why. Human beings are human beings regardless of their nationality. We all feel pain and joy. The joy part is fine; it is the pain that some of us suffer at the hands of some others which is bad. There are hospitals, schools, police, judiciary and probably every other department of government in underdeveloped countries just as there are in developed countries.

The only difference could be that they may not be working as efficiently or effectively. Their officials might be corrupt. A criminal commits an offence in a country ridden with corruption. This is what the victim may have to go through. The victim goes to the police station, the police ask for a bribe to register the case. Still the whole process may take many days. The police may even not register a case as they are free to act as they please and certainly free to accept a bribe from the offender. As discussed before there can never be just one corrupt person within an honest system; if there is one person asking for and accepting bribes openly, the whole system is corrupt from top to bottom. Within a corrupt system everything is buyable. So, a victim will have to bribe the police first, and not just once, but every time he or she goes to the police station. Then he will have to bribe the public prosecutor, to plead the case well. Still the offender is free to bribe the judge if the judge is corrupt. If anyone gets justice in a corrupt system, it can be for either of the two following reasons: firstly, their opponent did not have enough money to buy the system or secondly, the first reason prevailed. This is just one example. The media is filled with numerous examples of the corruption that takes place around us. Casual research will show us how deeply entrenched corruption is in many societies. Money in the form of paper currency changes hands at all these levels, where corrupt officials sell their souls for a very small sum of money every day. This is corruption. Its impact is that someone felt pain he or she did not deserve. Its impact is that someone had to wait for hours to reach hospital because an ambulance did not arrive on time, because there was no ambulance, because a government did not have enough tax revenue collection to have an ambulance service for its people, because corrupt tax officials took bribes from those who should have paid taxes.

An honest bottom cannot have a corrupt top

In countries where corruption is prevalent, the top and everyone from top to bottom is corrupt. There might be some exceptions, but they do not make a substantial impact either on the delivery of services or on reducing the level of corruption because their numbers are insignificant. A corrupt bottom is incapable of questioning a corrupt superior because when you are corrupt yourself, what moral standing do you have to question anyone? Secondly, if you are busy trying to fill your own pockets you don't care much about issues like honesty or integrity. So, this is what goes on in countries where the level of corruption is high. If you can get ten bucks in bribes a day you do that, if you can get

100 bucks a day you do that, if you can make 10,000 bucks a day you do that. The result is that everyone is corrupt and the big fish want to make and keep the small fish corrupt so they can themselves make big bucks by accepting kickbacks and deposit those in bank accounts present in secrecy jurisdictions with no one to question them. So, those who steal billions allow the ones who should have raised their voice and brought these big fish to justice to become corrupt, and that is how their voices get silenced forever.

Big fish make big bucks out of this corruption and lose their souls; small fish lose their souls for peanuts.

And who is going to bell the cat here?

Both the big and the small fish are causing pain to people. Let's see how small fish cause pain. This is just one example: a government department buys medicines for patients at a government hospital; the officials of that government hospital sell those medicines at a cheap price to privately owned drug stores situated right outside the hospital. Those medicines were meant for patients of a government hospital, and who goes to those hospitals in low-income countries? Those who are at the bottom of the ladder. So now these poor patients will have to buy the medicines they should have had for free. Who is making money? The small fish. And what is the big fish doing? We will come to that soon.

Some of you may ask why am I saying this without providing proof? If I provide you with some evidence it will still be me providing you with that piece of evidence. It will be what I know, not what you know.

I am not asking you to believe a word of this. You have absolutely every right to disagree with me. But disagree with me only after you have put some effort into finding out for yourself what is going on. If you disagree without that effort, then you will not be doing justice to yourself. In that case, your agreement or disagreement will based on nothing. Whichever way you go, make sure that your opinion is based on something solid. The next time you have some spare time, spend some of it investigating what is going on in your city. Searching the internet can be a starting point. Type the name of a country, a province or a city and add the word 'corruption' or a particular 'category of crime' and follow the leads, and you will at least be able to read something about the level of corruption and crime present in those places. Bear in mind every crime does not make it into the newspapers.

Now, how do these government officials who sell drugs to privately owned drug stores escape the auditors? They bribe them as well. In such countries, the whole chain from top to bottom is corrupt. Everyone gets a cut, right from the bottom to the top. Money here gets collected everywhere and at all levels and a percentage of it moves to the top. Everyone who is collecting bribes or receiving kickbacks is passing some money to the one above him or her. The whole chain is connected. What does a minister of government do, how does he make money? He obviously does not have the time to collect bribes or commissions from everyone in the chain. He collects it from the person sitting at the top of each chain, otherwise they get transferred and someone else who agrees to a certain amount every year or is ready to pay the amount upfront gets that job. After that he is free to make a profit, the clause being that the injustice should not be seen in the media and the paperwork has to look reasonably clean. If the paperwork does not look clean, it should not be in the public domain; government auditors can of course be bribed or transferred.

So how does the top, i.e. the political leadership, make money in countries with a high rate of corruption?

If a government has the discretion to make decisions in the absence of rules, that is a jackpot for them. They can do whatever they want to and there will be no one to question them, not even the courts. To reduce corruption at the top, everything that a government does must be done as per the country's regulations and not according to anyone's discretion. Discretion is the cause of corruption. Those regulations should not be in violation of any laws and should be in accordance with the principles of natural justice. Many countries, or perhaps all countries, declare the equality of everyone before the law. The concept of equality before the law presupposes the presence of law, which means a piece of legislation or regulations to deal with a particular situation. In the absence of that, situations will be dealt with in a discretionary way, so how will two or more entities get treated equally, either at the same time or at different times, when the regulations on how to handle situations are absent? It is certainly not possible. For equality of law for everyone, there have to be rules and regulations for every possible situation that may arise. The regulations should not allow anyone to exercise any level of discretion, as that will only give rise to corruption. All decisions can be made based on the facts of a case. To ensure equality of law, if a regulation does not exist on a particular subject then a decision should not be made until a regulation exists.

If they can play with the recruitment of new government employees, they will appoint those who bribe them – and imagine the employees who get a job after bribing someone: how honest are they going to be? If they can give a licence to someone to do a certain activity, to do mining or to conduct some other business within their jurisdiction, and have the money transferred to some bank account that is hard to find in some secrecy jurisdiction, they will do that. This all happens in the absence of rules and regulations or their poor enforcement. Enforcement is poor when the law enforcing agencies are not autonomous and cannot keep themselves insulated from pressures they have to deal with, including political pressures and when the courts take decades to deliver justice.

The list above is nothing compared to what they do. The big fish are happy that the small fish are corrupt and no one can question them. And the small fish are corrupt because of paper currency. If you take paper currency out of the equation, then there is a chance that the small fish will catch the big fish, and moreover the big fish will not be able to:

- Bribe investigators
- Bribe prosecutors
- Bribe judges
- Bribe witnesses
- Bribe someone to destroy the evidence
- Hire someone to harm any of the above.

They could still transfer money into an off-shore secrecy jurisdiction bank account from their off-shore bank account, but what good is that to anyone who lives in your jurisdiction? Eventually he or she will be caught because not every investigator, prosecutor or judge can have or make use of an off-shore bank account.

In organisations and countries where corruption is rampant, the most important criterion for promotion in a job is how much money you can push up the chain. Who can be concerned about improving the effectiveness or efficiency of the programmes when the criterion to excel is something else? People who have to deal with corrupt entities are at their mercy. Such organisations do not become user-friendly and their operations do not become effective or efficient because the criterion for career advancement of employees there is how much money they have collected in the form of bribes and kickbacks and pushed up the chain.

If corruption stops at the lower level, the employees working at the lower level will put a stop to the corruption taking place at the higher level. So, if the bottom is clean, you cannot have a dirty top. Honesty gives courage and strength to the human mind. An honest mind has the ability to fight against any number of dishonest people. A corrupt mind does not.

Corruption can take place in an infinite number of ways but they all derive comfort from the existence of paper currency. A new and different way to ask for a bribe or embezzle public funds can exist beyond what can be imagined. Economic development in a democracy demands price. The price is that the citizens have to keep their eyes open and work to keep the democratic values and the democracy itself alive. One of the reasons many countries in the world suffer from corruption is because a significant percentage of their citizens is not aware and is uneducated.

Trade brings economic development

Demand for goods and services runs the global economy. Our economy cannot survive without demand for goods and services. More people having the means to become consumers will help production go up, which will create additional employment opportunities. They could not become consumers because they did not have the resources to buy what you could produce, so additional quantities were not produced and so additional employment opportunities could not be generated in your part of the world. People living in a corruption-ridden country who do not buy goods manufactured in other countries could very well have become consumers. It is just because they are not producing enough and so they do not have the purchasing power to buy what you could sell to them. As discussed above, corruption in many countries is not letting these countries develop and is hampering the development of the whole world.

Financial crises like the ones we have seen could impact us that hard because we have not been able to realise the full economic potential that we are capable of. To explain this a bit more, let's say that there are two trees in this world, one of apples and the other one of guavas. They are owned by two separate entities. They trade with each other. Let's assume that the rest of the world eats grass which is available without any effort. Let's say that for some reason there were no apples on the apple tree this year. The impact would be felt by both the tree owners. There will be no trade. They will be facing a crisis that year, a global crisis, because it is just the two of them on the whole planet who were trading with each other. Now let's assume that the rest of us were also growing apples and guavas. Will one tree not producing fruit have any impact on the economy? Certainly it will not. This is because the size of economy would have grown so big that if a single entity stops production it does not have any impact on the economy. The heat generated by financial crises is felt partly because our economy is not as big as it could be. Vast populations living in India, China, South-East Asia, the Middle East, Africa and South America, which could contribute to the global economy firstly by becoming producers and then by becoming consumers, are not a part of it as yet. They are not contributing to their full potential either as producers or as consumers. Bringing those people in will make our economy stronger, more diverse and less prone to any global crises. To be brought in, they will require the investment of capital and development of infrastructure. If corrupt officials embezzle the funds meant for capital investment or infrastructure development, then bringing those people into the global economy as producers and consumers will take more time than it should. This implies that if the underdeveloped parts of the world do not develop quickly, we will be prone to terrorism, wars and financial crises on a global scale.

The utility of a product or service creates its own demand. As long as everyone is not producing the same commodity, trade is possible, which will result in the enhancement of the standard of living of people and an increase in the tax revenue of the state. If everyone is producing the same commodity there will not be any need for trade. For trade to take place, exchange of what I have with what you have and I need, is required. As long as someone is producing rice, someone is producing vegetables, someone is making instruments for agriculture, someone is running a cold storage facility, someone is producing fertilisers, someone is generating electricity, someone is building houses, someone is running a bank, someone is providing educational services, someone is providing leisure holidays, someone is ensuring security, someone is providing medical care – the list is endless – trade is possible and economic activity will go on and grow. As long as another entity is willing to sacrifice its resources to buy what you are offering, trade will take place and your production will work towards economic enhancement. It applies to entities trading within an economy and to entities trading between economies.

Elaborating on the principle discussed above that the utility of a product or service creates its own demand, let's take the example of the many electronic products we use today that were unheard of only a few years ago. The availability of these products created a demand for them because consumers found a utility in these products. Millions found employment in the industries that develop, manufacture and supply these products. Had people employed in these industries been involved in producing something more orthodox, they may not have created as much value for themselves and the economy. Or had these people not been creative and inventive and started manufacturing something for sale in an already saturated market, they would not have been able to create as much value. The key point is that there is always room to increase production within an economy. But everyone cannot start producing the commodity, more of which is not needed. The new entrants will have to bring in newer products and newer services that fill an unmet need for consumers. As long as consumers can get some utility out of a newly introduced product they may buy it. Supplying a product for which the market is already saturated may not help either the entity supplying the product or the economy to grow. For example, the demand for product X in an economy is 100 units and the current supply is 100 units. You create ten more units of that product and supply it to that market. When the demand is 100 and the supply is 110, ten units will remain unconsumed. This means that the investment of capital and labour might have produced more return had it been invested in some other sector. More supply may increase consumption in the short run, but in the long run more supply of that product or service may not increase consumption. This is because in the short run consumers may buy more products or services than they need, for consumption in the future. But in the long run, the consumption pattern of an entity is rigid. For example, a person can buy a book today and if there is a discount on the second one, this person may buy the discounted book as well. But in the long run, this person is going to buy only as many books as they can read.

To help an economy achieve its full potential and increase employment opportunities, new products and services with newer utility will have to be introduced. Flooding the market with additional quantities of previously available products or services will not cause an increase in consumption in the long run, but products or services with newer utilities may create demand for themselves.

The most important dimension is to find your competitive advantage. There can never be just one advantage you have today that will allow you to compete forever. The advantage you have today and that allows you to compete today, may not act as an advantage tomorrow in a world which is so inventive and becoming a global village for more of us by the day. At the micro and the macro level, i.e. at the level of an entity and an economy, you will have to constantly evolve and look for the advantage that will allow you to effectively compete against your competitors. You may either have to hone your existing competitive advantage or move into a completely new sphere. The factors that determine whether you hone your existing advantage or move into a new sphere are your capabilities and the surrounding environment. Not finding or exploiting your competitive advantage at the micro level will lead to underperformance; at the macro level it will lead to lower economic growth. On the other hand, finding and exploiting the factor that gives you an advantage against your competitors and which will allow you to compete effectively will lead to better performance at the micro level and higher economic growth at the macro level. A low-income economy may have 'less expensive labour' as its competitive advantage. It is for the high-income economies to figure out what will act as their competitive advantage, considering that they have many more resources than low-income economies.

Have the high-income economies utilised their resources to find and exploit their competitive advantage or are they just blaming the low-income economies for offering less expensive labour? Have the high-income economies created conditions to train their populace towards acquiring a competitive advantage?

Development has to be sustainable

As the world is developing and development spreads to the under-developed parts of the world, demand for goods and services will increase in those parts of the world. It is undoubtedly good for the world and the world economy. It will make life easier for the human beings living in those parts of the world and the global economy will expand. New markets will develop, increasing employment every-where. But we cannot consume all the resources that this beautiful planet of ours has offered to us. It is only by adopting sustainable developmental practices that the development of the whole world in the long run is possible without us having to give up our way of life. Development that is not sustainable will be short lived. As our numbers are increasing every day, it is necessary that only sustainable development practices are adopted. Otherwise the phase of develop-ment and peace will be a tiny fraction of the history of humankind. We cannot consume everything that we have today and leave nothing for tomorrow. Imagine having used all the petroleum, iron ore, coal and uranium that we have within the next ten years, and imagine how the world will be without that. What sort of development can you imagine without these natural resources? Expand the list of resources mentioned above. Whatever resource that we have, it is not infinite. The quantity of any resource, whether known or unknown, is limited. So, to stay developed forever and enjoy the benefits of development, we have no other option but to adopt development practices that are sustainable in the long run.

The practice of returning to nature what you have taken from it is the way to go. The planting and raising of just one tree every year can be the start of a contribution. The importance of recycling cannot be underestimated. Without recycling we are reducing our resources. If the cost of recycling is high somewhere, the recyclable material can be sent to another location where it could be recycled at a lesser cost. Governments, in order to promote sustainable developmental practices, will have to take the initiative by providing tax benefits to entities that research and adopt sustainable developmental practices.

2 Corruption no more

Corruption is an offence in all the countries around the world. When a government official in any country, be it a developed country or a developing one, asks for a bribe, what gives him comfort? It is the fact that he thinks that he will not be caught because no one is watching. Many other factors could provide comfort to such a person. His superiors could also be corrupt, so he is not worried about anyone making any complaints. But then what is providing comfort to his or her superiors and their superiors, if they are all corrupt? It is the fact that when they accepted the bribe money they knew that this was not visible to anyone except the receiver and the giver. This fact provides a big psychological comfort to every bribe taker, whether it is a traffic policeman or any other corrupt official, working in either a government or non-government sector. So, what can be done? The answer is simple: take their comfort away; if the movement of money between entities becomes visible, corruption will end. How can that happen?

All the accepters of bribes and kickbacks know that they can always deny that they accepted any bribe or kickbacks. Proving that they accepted any bribe money can be very difficult when it comes to officials well versed in the innovative techniques of corruption. So, the solution to this menace of corruption is to take the comfort of these corrupt officials away: prohibit the use of paper currency and make it mandatory within your jurisdiction that all transfers of money to settle transactions will take place electronically between bank accounts. That means money will travel only between bank accounts to settle transactions and for every other purpose for which paper currency is being used today and it will be replaced by electronic currency.

Make the use of paper currency a thing of the past. Perhaps it would have been difficult to do this a few decades back; but today it is possible. If paper currency is replaced by a system where payments of money are made electronically from one bank account to another then the monetary transactions between entities, whether they are natural or artificial, will be visible. All transfers of money between entities will be via their bank accounts. The transfer of money electronically will leave a visible trail for every transfer from one entity and bank account to another. Money transferred from anywhere to anywhere and from anyone to anyone will be visible, including the use of money. For example, Entity A from Country J sends money to Entity B in Country Y. Entity B goes to a car dealer and buys a car. The car dealer uses that money to buy a truck. The truck seller uses that money to go on a world tour. All those transactions will be visible in totality. Many of us today are transferring money electronically to make payments and these details are available and visible to banks. What this transition to a paper currency-free economy will do is make the movement of money between all entities visible. This will directly check corruption and have an impact on many antisocial activities that happen in any society. The transition to a paper currency-free economy where payments are made electronically will have a direct impact on the crime graph in any country. Bank robberies or other thefts involving money will simply not happen. Demands for ransoms will disappear. The movement of entities wanted by the police will be more visible. The sellers of contraband and professional criminals will find it hard to sell contraband and carry on their trade and so will not be able to harm humanity.

The transition to a paper currency-free economy is dependent on many other factors. Surely the last few sentences will have given rise to a lot of questions. One question would certainly have been if it is possible at all. Possible, certainly, but a few changes may be needed to our existing legal and banking systems and infrastructure. But why should we do it? The reason is simple. It is for the benefits that it will bring to all of us. Imagine your kids not being able to buy drugs, or the inability of an entity to sell its contraband, or a criminal not being able to traffic young women and children for the sex trade, or someone who wants to harm your society not being able to do so.

All that and much more can be achieved if we move towards a paper currency-free environment, although the transition must have an emphasis on its ability to reduce crime and corruption otherwise the effort will not yield the desired results. Obtaining the results of 'no corruption' and 'no professional crime' from this transition is easy; it is just like a by-product that is bound to be born with a little effort, but if that little effort to reduce crime and corruption is not put in, then the transition to a paper currency-free environment can still take place but it will not result in reduced corruption and crime.

We are moving towards a time where the use of paper currency will decrease. If paper currency is allowed to settle even a small percentage of transactions in an economy, then the benefits of a paper currency-free economy will not be realised because if there is any paper currency available, it will be used for unlawful activities such as demanding bribes, selling contraband or other criminal activities. People who intend to indulge in unlawful activities without leaving a visible trail would use paper currency. So, for all the benefits to be realised it is imperative that the use of paper currency is prohibited by law. The transition to a paper currency-free economy will ensure that movement of money between entities is visible.

The transition to prohibit the use of paper currency will not be a natural process. The government of a country intending to make this transition will have to actively make that decision. They will have to make it mandatory by law that all transfers of money within its jurisdiction will be made electronically from one bank account to another and that no paper currency, either domestic or foreign, will be used within its jurisdiction. If the use of a foreign paper currency is not prohibited by law, then some entities may start accepting foreign paper currency in order to keep their transactions hidden from the eyes of the law. Some countries may have laws that allow debts to be settled in any currency prevalent in the world; such laws will have to be amended for this transition to function smoothly and bring the desired results.

On which activities public money was spent, how much was spent and when was it spent etc., all such details, will become visible. It is possible that some government departments may have a policy that all payments for the procurement of goods or services are to be made by transferring money from the government bank account, but this still leaves room for kickbacks to be accepted in cash. The acceptance of kickbacks will be visible and easier to prove when the use of paper currency is prohibited by law and money is transferred only electronically. It is only then that corrupt officials will be scared of accepting kickbacks, and if they do accept kickbacks the details will be visible. This gives rise to a question as to why can a corrupt official not demand bribes or kickbacks be transferred into his or her bank account? The answer is that proving corruption took place will be easier. The bribe giver or others will be in a much better place to prove that they were compelled to give a bribe because money will be moving between the bank accounts of the giver and the taker of the bribe, and it will make it much easier for the bribe giver to prove that he had to pay a bribe. It will be easy to bring the corrupt to justice. Corrupt officials in any country will find it hard to indulge in corruption, firstly because the electronic transfer of money will not be as easy as the transfer of paper currency, and secondly because the electronic transfer of money will leave a visible trail, i.e. money transferred from one account to another will be visible.

Some entities may try to make an innocent person look corrupt by transferring money into their bank account and later alleging corruption. All someone will need to do is to deposit some money into someone's bank account and then allege that that person demanded a bribe. If that person holds a position of authority and you deal with this person, then he or she will not have too many defences to rely upon to prove his or her innocence. The safeguard that can be used against this is that banks may not transfer money into any bank account without approval from the account holder. Banks can keep all this money in some account specifically created for this purpose and transfer the money only when the approval from the account holder is obtained. For example, Entity A deposits money into the bank account of Entity B. Entity B's bank accepts that money from Entity A but does not transfer it into Entity B's bank account without approval from Entity B. This will ensure that no one is falsely made to look corrupt; such an option could be given to all account holders by banks.

Impact of transition on corruption

Corruption happens in a number of ways. One is when entities have to bribe government officials to get legitimate jobs done, e.g. obtaining a licence to start a business at a time when they have fulfilled all the requirements but officials are demanding bribes to grant the required licence. In many countries where corruption is rampant, the residents cannot even get a driver's licence without bribing corrupt government officials.

A second is when people can bribe a government official to get an illegal job done, e.g. an entity is able to obtain a licence without complying with any of the legal requirements. It may not stop at just obtaining a licence without meeting the requirements. Imagine someone being able to get anything done just because of the money they have. What a scary society it will be to live in. Would you expect justice there? Would you want to live there?

A third way corruption happens is when public money is misused, i.e. when the money allocated to be spent on public projects is misused by government officials. One way that can happen is when a government official who is responsible for the procurement of goods or services awards the contract to someone who offers the highest kickbacks. With the current system of paper currency being in existence, proving that kickbacks have been received can be very difficult for any agency because there is no visible transfer of money from one entity to the other. With electronic payments involving bank accounts being the only medium of payment, it will become quicker and easier to see whom the goods were purchased from, what goods were purchased, the location and legal status of the selling business, the comparative market value of the purchase, whether the funds were spent on their intended purpose, and how much money was paid to whom, and when.

Let me tell you a story I heard from someone some time back. A few corrupt officials in some country, in order to embezzle public funds, decided to have an artificial pond constructed in front of their building to beautify the surroundings. All the paperwork was completed, including the invoices from builders and suppliers, and no one could find any fault with it. The funds were embezzled; everyone got his or her share but the pond was never built. A new supervisor was posted to that unit and was surprised to see that as per the documents a pond was built and the money was spent but he could not see any pond. His inquiries revealed the truth to him. So, he and the rest of his team decided to deconstruct the pool and bring the land back to its original shape as the pond had become a breeding ground for mosquitoes. So, public money was spent twice: once to construct the pond and once to deconstruct the pond – which was never built in the first place. Do you think that these leeches would have accepted kickbacks into their bank accounts? What gave them comfort is the paper currency we use.

With electronic currency being the only means of payment, the utilisation of public funds will be visible. If the movement of public funds could be watched, the embezzlement of public funds will end. This will be a big boost to development. It is not how much money is spent but how much money reaches the intended quarter that determines the level of development. Corruption siphons money out of a system and slows development down. The fact that money should reach the intended quarter is as important as the allocation. For example, the government of a country allocates resources for building an irrigation system. When the irrigation system is built, the region will take a step forward towards development. If the money ends up in the pockets of some corrupt officials the region will remain underdeveloped as before. With electronic currency, governments and their agencies will be able to watch how, when and on which items their officials spend allocated funds. The transactions between government departments and suppliers will be visible. Electronic payments will leave behind a visible, auditable trail, e.g. the government authorised the expenditure to buy ten trucks. With payment being made electronically it will be easier to find out whom the payment was made to, how much was paid, when was it paid, the business details of the seller, whether the business was a public entity or a proprietary company etc. An analysis of the bank accounts of the officials involved will also reveal if they accepted any kickbacks for awarding any contract while spending the public funds. Today kickbacks can be accepted in the form of cash without leaving any visible trail for anyone.

The transition may not make the system totally corruption free but will make it difficult to commit a fraud. The chances of committing a fraud where there is no paper currency will depend on the strength and effectiveness of governance exercised by a government, the strength of checks and balances and the independence of the auditors etc. It is quite possible that some corrupt officials may get kickbacks in kind or may get the money transferred into a bank account under a fake identity. But a bank transfer will be easier to see and so would a transfer of property that is required to be registered. For example, when a corrupt official receives a car or a house in return for a favour, such a transfer will be visible upon registration of the house or car.

Impact of transition on economic development

The corruption within government departments has the biggest impact on a country's development. Corrupt government officials embezzle public funds that are allocated for developmental activities. They do this by accepting kickbacks when awarding contracts and also by directly embezzling the money. Corrupt officials can embezzle public funds even without the presence of a supplier, for example by creating fake suppliers and fake receipts. Government officials ask for and accept bribe money from members of the public for any legitimate jobs they have to do as part of their work or for doing illegitimate jobs that they are not supposed to do. The first type mentioned above has an impact on the development of a country, for example when public funds allocated for building of schools, hospitals, roads etc. are embezzled. This has a direct impact on a country's development. The second type is when a government official asks for a bribe to do something that he should not do. For example, a policeman does not catch a trafficker of young women and children after accepting a bribe or a government official gives a favour to someone who does not qualify.

The non-availability of paper currency would reduce corruption, as corrupt officials will be scared of having money transferred into their bank accounts due to it increasing the chances of them being caught. The transfer of money via electronic means makes it easy to watch its movement between different accounts. And if a corrupt official demands a bribe, it will be very easy for the bribe giver to complain and prove that complaint. Proving an incident of corruption with the paper currency in use is comparatively more difficult than with electronic currency. The transfer of money between accounts will be totally visible if a transition to a paper currency-free economy takes place.

Corruption reduces the economic activity in any economy by reducing the disposable income of its citizens. This is because when people spend their money on paying bribes they are left with less for other purposes. By reducing corruption, disposable income will increase, which will increase the economic activity within an economy. Some extra money in the hands of more people means more economic activity and gives rise to more commerce. A lot of money in the hands of a few people will not increase economic activity as much as some money in the hands of lots of people. This is because there is a limit to what we need. Let's say that there is this person with 100,000,000 dollars. How many cars, how many televisions, how many houses, how many holidays etc. would he want to have? Now let's imagine that there are 1,000 people with 100,000 dollars each. They will all want to have cars, televisions, houses, vacations etc. This will give rise to lots of economic activity and generate employment. This is just an example to prove that more money in the hands of more people increases economic activity. Everyone has the right to make as much money as they can within the bounds of the law. Entrepreneurship has to be encouraged. A reduction in economic activity will lead to a reduction in employment. On the same count, an increase in disposable income will increase economic activity, which will generate employment. So, a reduction in corruption will fuel the growth of economic development and increase employment.

Prohibiting the use of paper currency will reduce corruption and crime in all parts of the world. However, even if the use of paper currency is prohibited and a transition is made towards electronic means to settle debts and make payments, some corrupt officials may ask for kickbacks in kind. But how many cars or other tangible goods can one have? Receiving money after you sell those objects will leave a visible and identifiable trail. In many countries entities have to bribe government officials even to get legitimate things done. The transition to a paper currency-free economy will make it difficult for corrupt officials to accept bribes.

All countries have seen scams and frauds, without exception. It is not possible to imagine a single country where public money has not been used by public officials for their own benefit. As long as paper currency stays as a medium, corruption and crime can exist and finding the culprits can be a hard job.

The transition to a paper currency-free economy cannot and should not be an overnight process. The time to complete the transition will depend on a number of factors, and it is only after that time has been taken into consideration that a time frame can be given to complete the transition.

How are payments made after transition to a paper currency-free economy?

When we discuss how payments are made after transition to a paper currency-free economy, we will also discuss how they are not allowed to be made under the law.

- Payments are allowed to be made electronically from one bank account to another, whether both accounts are present within your jurisdiction or one account is in a foreign jurisdiction. Payments from foreign bank accounts, either over the internet or with the use of foreign-issued debit or credit cards, will have to be allowed to settle transactions to ensure ease of making payments. Secondly, the identity of the receiver of the money within your jurisdiction will be visible to you even if the identity of the payer is not.
- Your local electronic currency replaces your local paper currency.
- If transition is partial then the currency notes kept are also used to make payments and settle transactions.
- What is explicitly prohibited by law is the use of any paper currency notes, including your paper currency that has been recalled and any foreign paper currency, to settle a transaction if that is not already the case.

Transfer of money

After transition to a paper currency-free economy, the paper currency will not be used within your jurisdiction and banks will not accept or give paper currency notes to anyone. It must be mandated by law that the balance of any bank account within your jurisdiction can change only when:

- Money is transferred electronically from one bank account to another, whether both accounts are within your jurisdiction or one is in a foreign jurisdiction
- In the event of a partial transition, an account balance is given a debit or credit for the withdrawal or deposit of paper currency notes that are still in circulation
- An account balance is given a credit for depositing a foreign paper currency
- An account balance is debited for withdrawing foreign paper currency.

This should apply to all bank accounts after the transition has been made, either complete or partial. This also requires that the banks should not have the ability to accept the recalled paper currency after a certain date, i.e. the government will have to specify a date by which all the paper currency present within an economy should be deposited into the banks. After this date, no bank should be able to accept the recalled paper currency and increase any entity's bank account balance as a result of the deposit of this currency. The banks after this date should not have the ability to give the recalled paper currency to any entity. Banks, however, should be allowed to change an entity's account balance as a result of the deposit or withdrawal of foreign paper currency; the facility to deposit or withdraw foreign currency may only be available at selected locations.

The use of fake currency

The easiest way to be rich is to find or invent a machine that could print paper currency; of course it depends on your ability to steal or create. Why would you worry about working? Just press the button and you could buy the whole world. Many antisocial entities try to print and smuggle fake currency. The reasons for their motivation can be many. Under the present system, any number of fake currency notes can be smuggled into an economy and the people who accept them may not be able to easily verify whether they are real or fake. This is because when you accept a currency note from someone, you look at the note but may not have the means or time to verify whether it is real or fake. But one thing that is certain is that fake currency in any economy is not doing any good. If fake currency is brought into an economy in very large amounts it can cause that economy to crash. Now if the use of paper currency notes is prohibited by law, what use will it be to anyone to bring fake currency notes into an economy? The impact of stopping the use of paper currency is that there will be no fake currency. The fear of hostile forces flooding an economy with fake currency will be gone. The chance that some currency smugglers could print fake currency and bring it into the economy will no longer exist.

The cost of printing currency will also disappear because there will be no need to print any currency. The cost of protecting your currency against counterfeit currency may not disappear totally, but should reduce substantially. Governments spend millions on protecting their currencies against fake currencies; with the paper currency gone, physical policing may no longer be necessary.

Our fight against crime

For centuries, we have been trying to fight crime. Criminals commit crime and then try to hide. Their belief that they will be able to hide after committing the crime gives them comfort. Once they start believing that they will not be able to hide and their comfort goes away, the crime rate will fall. The transition to a paper currency-free economy will have a very big impact on fighting crime. The movement of people wanted by the law will be visible because they will need to spend money to fulfil their daily needs. Let's look at this example. Entity A is accused of committing a crime. They are wanted by the law. Now, to purchase something Entity A needs to transfer money to the seller's bank account, either electronically or by cheque. When Entity A makes any purchase, it will be visible. The possibility of tracing Entity A will increase. This will help bring people wanted by the law to justice as it will provide information about their whereabouts. Criminals who commit crime for money will find it hard to continue their business. The transactions between these criminals and their clients involving the transfer of money will be visible. For example, Entity A pays Entity B to do an unlawful act. If the payment is made by transferring money electronically from one bank account to the other, then it will be visible. Organised professional criminals will find it hard to operate (of course, tracking the movement of a person is dependent on establishing the identity of that person).

On television some time back there was a clip from a movie in which some bank robbers threw a lot of cash on a freeway. We are not totally alien to news of cash robberies in the middle of the night. The physical paper currency attracts them. Had we stopped using paper currency in totality, a bank robbery or any robbery of physical cash would not be possible, at least by the burglars who believe in muscle power. For those who believe in brain power, the details mentioned below should make it difficult for them as well. In a paper currency-free economy, the money transferred from one account to another is visible and any bank robbery is impossible.

Our right to privacy of information

The transition to a paper currency-free economy will empower law enforcement agencies to view the financial transactions of entities. How much of this information should be visible, to whom, and what procedures should be followed to view anyone's spending and income are to be decided by the government of a country and its citizens. Undoubtedly this is debateable. What is not debateable is that no society would want its criminals to not be caught and be free to roam at large. So, who will have the authority to look inside an entity's bank account? Who will authorise that and what procedures need to be put in place? These are the questions that need serious discussion if they have not already been answered. Leaving these questions unanswered and not putting well-defined procedures in place will cause chaos. It should be a prerequisite to transition that these questions are answered and detailed procedures are established with regard to viewing the information relating to an entity's income and spending.

We have to create a balance between our right to privacy of our information and someone's ability to commit:

- Acts of terrorism
- Illegal human trafficking
- Corruption
- Money laundering
- Sales of contraband drugs and weapons
- Prostitution of children
- Prostitution against someone's wishes
- Child pornography
- The unlawful sale and purchase of human organs
- Every other criminal offence that causes pain to people through no fault of their own.

We cannot have a blanket ban to protect our privacy and still expect our city, community or country to be free from corruption and crime. Such a blanket ban will only support and embolden criminals to commit the crimes mentioned above, plus many more, with no fear of being caught. Nobody would be able to see what criminals do and thus be able to bring them to justice. A blanket ban would provide psychological comfort to criminals, empower them and only strengthen their ability to give pain to people; they will commit crimes for their own material benefit to the detriment of the rest of us. So, we have to have a balance between our right to privacy of information and the ability of law enforcement agencies to look at the activities and transactions of antisocial elements.

The ability of law enforcement agencies depends on their ability to see what antisocial elements do and how they do it. So, if we expect these antisocial elements to be caught and not to harm us, then we have to have a balance between our right to privacy of our information and the ability of law enforcement agencies to see what these criminals are doing.

It comes down to answering a few questions:

1. Who can see the information?
2. Whose information can be seen?
3. What information can be seen?
4. When can that information be seen?
5. Who can authorise the viewing of that information?
6. After the law enforcement agencies have seen that information, who else can be shown it for the purpose of administration of justice?
7. What procedures need to be put in place so that there is no leakage of this information and it is viewed only by those who are intended by law to see it.

In the majority of countries today (perhaps all), law enforcement agencies can obtain a search warrant for a premises if they want to ensure that someone is not committing a crime there. They have this authority so that they can catch criminals and we can live in peace. The same principles and procedures can be applied before any law enforcement agency can look at the details and transactions of any entity's bank account. So, this is not new – it has been in existence for a long time.

This can be part of the legislation or regulations governing criminal investigation that a bank will not show the details or transactions of a bank account, or the details of all those who have transferred money into that bank account, or of bank accounts into which money has been transferred unless directed by a court of law. So here you have put the onus on the banks to protect your privacy and you have also created checks and balances by authorising only the courts of law to direct the banks to provide that information to law enforcement agencies when they are investigating crimes. Some of us may ask what if you urgently need to look at a certain bank account in order to catch a criminal or to prevent a criminal from harming the community? In that event, there is nothing stopping us from having a magistrate or a judge on duty 24/7 to deal with those specific situations.

We cannot have a blanket ban and expect to live in peace.

The sellers of contraband

Entities selling contraband are not doing any good to society; they are causing harm. It may never be that just one entity is selling the contraband in isolation; generally they would be part of a bigger syndicate. Let's look at this example: a user of recreational drugs is not going to buy a million dollars' worth of drugs in one go. Most consumers of drugs spend some amount on a weekly or daily basis. Most of them would buy drugs off the street clandestinely. A street drug seller buys from someone else, who buys from someone else and so on. Eventually a percentage of what someone paid to the street drug seller ends up in the hands of the entities sitting at the top of the chain.

The street sellers of contraband know that the transactions between them and their customers can remain hidden because the transfer of paper currency does not leave a visible signature. Continuing with the example of drugs, a drug seller is not going to sell a million dollars' worth of drugs to anyone in one go; they probably need to find tens of buyers and sell them some drugs every week. The transfer of drugs in exchange for currency notes does not leave any visible proof of the transaction, which is not visible to anyone except the buyer and the seller. How can their activities be made visible? By transitioning to the use of electronic means for all payments and transfers of money and by stopping the use of paper currency within an economy. The production of drugs will stop at its origin when people stop buying drugs. Drug dealing is a business that exists because of paper currency. Without paper currency, this business will find it very difficult to continue. No matter how big a group of drug sellers is, to survive it needs to sell the drugs to ordinary people and in big numbers. In most countries selling recreational drugs and narcotics is illegal. When someone buys such drugs, they give the drug seller some paper currency notes and get the contraband drugs. Imagine giving a bank cheque to a drug seller or transferring money to their bank account electronically. Will the drug seller accept it? Certainly, they will not. But let's say that the drug seller does accept it. What will that drug seller say about what they were selling? Thirdly, the transaction will be viewable to law enforcement agencies. Drug selling is not a small issue. It is not just about selling a few bucks' worth of drugs to anyone.

Are contraband dealers or professional criminals going to declare their income in their annual tax return? They are not. So, what are they going to do with the drug money? The answer can be left to your imagination because anything that can be imagined they will do it. But of course, they will keep it hidden from the law because once it is declared, a government can question the source of that money. And paper currency notes facilitate that. How would a drug dealer be able to sell drugs when his options are either to accept a cheque or go for a direct electronic transfer? Let's take this example, where 100,000 people (which is a very conservatively selected figure) living within an economy buy drugs worth fifty dollars every week (which is again a conservatively selected figure), spending $260 million over a year (100,000 × $50 × 52 weeks). This money is dirty money. Probably a big percentage of this money is not going to enter the system for a legitimate purpose. Imagine this money in the hands of someone at the top of a drug chain every year. When the transition to a paper currency-free economy takes place, transactions will become hard to carry out at the bottom level and money will not flow to the upper echelons of those chains of contraband sellers. No selling and buying of drugs will clean up our streets and some of the crime that exists in our society. An analysis of the flow of money will also reveal the entities present at various levels within the chain.

Collection of tax revenue

Most modern-day governments fund their activities from the tax revenue they collect. The difference between revenue and expenditure determines deficit or surplus. The more money a government has, the more it can spend on public welfare. Currently, with paper currency in existence, it is possible for an entity to not declare all of its revenue and avoid the payment of some or all of the taxes it should be paying. For example, an entity runs a business, someone pays this entity in cash; it may be up to this entity if it reports this cash as revenue or not. Regardless of the size of the entity, the present system, where paper currency can be used to make payments and settle debts, provides an opportunity to entities to report their revenue and expenditure as per their comfort, just because they can do that.

The transition to make and receive payments solely by electronic methods will take that ability away from all entities because the revenue and expenditure transactions will be visible to taxation authorities. The transition will help reduce the amount of black money within an economy. Again, how much information is visible, to whom, and what procedures are required to view that information are issues to be decided by the government and citizens of each country.

The collection of additional tax revenue will make governments financially stronger and able to spend more money on sectors such as education, infrastructure and public health etc. Entities within an economy will be compelled to declare their true revenue and expenditure. This collection of additional tax revenue will not come from any increase in tax rates; it is just that now the tax authorities will be able to see all the transactions of a business, and entities will not be able to keep their true revenue and expenditure figures hidden any more.

Solutions for the visually impaired, elderly and those who may lack literacy

Paper currency notes have distinguishing features for people who are visually impaired. The elderly may also need some help at times to figure out how much money they have spent. Those who are illiterate will need to have some basic literacy skills to know how much money has been transferred into their bank account and how much they have spent. Without those basic skills, the illiterate will not be able to understand the system fully and might also be vulnerable to fraud. The following as a minimum should be done before transition:

1. Braille printing machines should be available at selected sale points for visually impaired people. They should be funded by the government and not be left to businesses to provide due to the additional costs they would incur
2. An automated phone call to the visually impaired, elderly, illiterate or others who may request this, after every transfer of money into or out of their bank account informing them about the transfer of money
3. An SMS text message, if requested by the account holder, after every transfer of money out of or into their bank account.

This should be done in addition to what exists at present and what may be required to be a necessity or convenience in future. An automated phone call or SMS can be connected to a transfer of money into or out of a bank account. An SMS will not suffice for visually impaired people, so they will require a phone call.

The threat of digital fraud

The question is, will we stop using debit cards or credit cards or stop making online payments if we do not go for a complete transition to a paper currency-free economy? The fact is that we are going to use these methods regardless of whether we get rid of paper currency. In all countries, the percentage of transactions settled by using bank cards or online bank transfers is only going to increase whether we go for this transition or not, and if paper currency is still used along with other means to make payments or transfer money then the corrupt and the criminal who want to keep their transactions hidden will use it. We are never going to say that we will not use bank cards or make payments online; debit and credit cards and other online payment mechanisms are here to stay.

So, the question is how much more risk of digital fraud will there be if we make a transition to a paper currency-free economy? Because we have to remember that this risk is not new; it is already present today. A transition to a paper currency-free economy will not bring this risk with it as something new or unknown to us; however, it may increase the amount of digital fraud because money will only be in online bank accounts.

In developed countries, there may not be an increase in the total number of bank accounts, though some debit cards for children may have to be connected to specified bank accounts. To protect those bank accounts there can be maximum daily transfer and spending limits set on the cards, and they may also not have any ability to be used online. This will work like a child having five or ten bucks in his or her pocket.

In countries still developing the number of bank accounts and debit cards connected to those will increase, as many people there may not currently have a bank account. For the protection of those people whose understanding of the banking system might be very limited, their debit cards can be made to be used only at payment terminals, with no capability to be used for online transactions. So, if anyone steals their bank account details, they will not be able to make any use of the information and only the account holder who has the debit card will be able to use it or get it cancelled if lost or stolen.

The question of the threat of digital fraud has to be answered in the light of the plusses and minuses of making a transition to a paper currency-free economy. The plusses include, but are not limited to, a reduction in:

- The ability of entities to give and receive bribes and kickbacks
- The ability of entities to commit crime for money
- The sale of illegal drugs and weapons
- Money laundering
- Human trafficking
- Child prostitution
- Forced prostitution
- The illegal sale and purchase of human organs
- The ability of terrorists to kill innocent people.

How strongly the checks mentioned above are enforced depends on a few factors being present in individual countries, some of them being:

- Political will
- The ability of investigating agencies, including their ability to keep themselves insulated from various pressures they may face while doing their job
- The speed with which the judiciary decides cases.

The threat of digital fraud arising from the transition to a paper currency-free economy must be looked at in context with the fact that we will never go back to a time when there will be no debit or credit cards or online payment mechanisms, whether we make the transition to paper currency-free economies or not.

The threat of digital fraud – cont'd

It is pertinent to discuss some of the possible checks to reduce or stop digital financial fraud. But what needs to be understood here is that if a thief can bulldoze a wall then the strength of the lock or the door is irrelevant. For example, if a fraudster no longer relies on fraudulently obtaining bank account details to transfer money to their account or to purchase something, but hacks a website or the whole system, then different measures will have to be put in place to stop them and bring them to justice.

The following discussion deals with those who fraudulently acquire the bank account details of people and use the information either to transfer money into their bank accounts or to make purchases.

The following check can be created to deter a fraudster from causing a damage. A time gap of a certain duration can be set on all transfers of money online or on transfers above a certain amount, whether the transfer is domestic or international (this includes purchases made online where an account holder requests their bank to transfer funds from their account to the seller's bank account). So, when money is requested to be transferred online, the account holder receives an SMS or an automated phone call to their nominated phone number informing them that they have a certain period of time to cancel the proposed transfer of funds and if they do not stop it, the funds will be transferred after that period of time. Here the account holder will not need to do anything if they have requested the transfer of funds and will not have to bear any additional load, but if someone has committed a fraud then the account holder will be able to stop the transaction. Such options can be standard for all transfers of money or just for those above a certain amount unless otherwise directed by the account holder. Procedures may have to be put in place to lift time gaps if the account holder requires the payments to be sent without a time gap.

The above model of a time gap between the request for a transfer of money and the actual transfer can apply to both:

a. The requests initiated by the account holder. Requests initiated by account holders are those where the account holder is transferring money online to other bank accounts from their own account
b. The requests initiated by others
    i.   Requests initiated by others are those where entities other than the account holder request the latter's bank to transfer money into their bank account, for example direct debit requests.
    ii. When a time gap becomes the norm, requests for direct debits will start to originate at the time of payment minus the time gap. For example, if the time gap is six hours and the time for payment of a bill is 3pm, the request for the direct debit will be made at 9am and the money will be transferred by the bank at 3pm, provided it does not receive any communication between 9am and 3pm from the account holder to stop that payment. The duration of the time gap can be up to 24 hours, which will provide enough time for an account holder to cancel a fraudulent request for a payment.

To protect people who have limited literacy skills or whose understanding of banking and online banking systems is limited:

a. The debit cards issued to them may not have any online usability
b. The usability of those debit cards may be restricted to paying for a purchase at an electronic payments terminal because people who

are not very banking literate are not going to use online banking from the beginning

c.   The debit cards issued to this group may only be usable within a certain geographical area. The use can be expanded beyond that geographical area upon the request of the account holder or nominated user. This will make it futile for fraudsters to steal the details of bank accounts present within your jurisdiction.

It is also important that all incidents of fraud are investigated, whether big or small. Incidents of financial fraud involving small amounts should not be left uninvestigated purely because the amount involved is small. This behaviour encourages low-level fraudsters to believe that as long as they commit frauds under a certain amount they are safe, and if such behaviour continues it will only encourage them to continue to commit frauds.

The transition does not need smartphones or computers

The transition to a paper currency-free economy should not be confused with the use of smartphones or the ability to make payments online; these are optional. It simply needs two things:

1.   The means with which a buyer of goods or services can transfer money from their bank account to the seller's bank account, i.e. a debit card or credit card
2.   The means with which a seller can receive money from the buyer's bank account to their bank account, i.e. an electronic payment terminal.

It has to be understood that no government can compel people to have smartphones or mobile phones; many people may not want to own a mobile phone, and phones may not be working at a particular point in time. So, what will these phoneless people do – not buy what they need? That is not the answer. Cash will disappear and be replaced with a bank card, which is connected to that person's bank account; when that person swipes, inserts or taps that card to make a payment, an amount equal to the purchase amount is debited from their bank account and is credited to the bank account of the seller. So, all you need is bank cards, and for bank cards to be used you need payment terminals, which are part of the infrastructure governments need to put in place before becoming a cash-free economy.

Mobile, wireless payment terminals are available today, so a new invention is not needed.

The use of computers, smartphones or other gadgets that can be used for payments and the transfer of money is purely optional, and cannot be a mandatory requirement for the transition to a paper currency-free economy. Also, if mobile phones can gain access to a network for payments in a particular area, so should the payment terminals. The presence of payment terminals in the hands of the sellers and bank cards in the hands of the buyers will make the transition smooth and easy for everyone.

The use of online banking is optional. So, those people who only use cash today will need to have a bank card connected to their bank accounts, and the sellers who only accept cash will need to have a device which transfers money from the bank account connected to the bank card to the bank account connected to the device when requested. Employers can still pay their employees by visiting the branch of a bank or by giving them a cheque. Whether people use online banking applications is up to them and cannot be a mandatory requirement for the transition to a paper currency-free economy; they can all still go to the branch of a bank as they do today.

It is, however, a mandatory requirement that the above-mentioned devices are operational when required by a seller of goods and services otherwise it will have a huge negative impact on the ability of businesses to survive, since they will not be able to sell their goods or services. Consequently, their country's GDP sold and tax revenue of their government would decline. When production is generated but is not sold, it is clearly a waste of the resources used to produce them. For example, a potter makes pitchers: if his pitchers are sold then he can buy the other commodities he needs, but if his pitchers are not sold then he cannot buy anything and all the resources used to make the pitchers, including labour, were wasted. Similarly, when the entities engaged in production in your country cannot sell what they produce, the amount of GDP sold will decrease, having a negative effect on the financial health of entities engaged in production and the economy. So, the payment terminals must always be operational when required by a seller of goods or services.

You can travel alone

Is a worldwide movement needed for the transition to a paper currency-free economy or can the government of any individual country act on its own? Why a worldwide movement? I want my own house to be in order – why would I care for the rest of the world to wake up? This transition can take place without the whole world joining in. Any government can recall its paper currency, prohibit the use of paper currency and make it mandatory that all transactions within its jurisdiction are settled electronically.

When you go for a transition towards a paper currency-free economy, how do people who visit your country settle transactions? When foreign entities enter your country, how do they pay their bills? Do they need to go to a bank just after they land at the airport or do they get bank accounts opened at the airport? These are some of the questions that will arise. A whole heap of solutions exists.

The answer is that they will pretty much do as they do today, with one exception. Today when someone visits your country, they have the following options:

- Transfer money electronically between bank accounts
- Use debit or credit cards that are acceptable in your country
- Exchange foreign paper currency for your paper currency
- Exchange traveller's cheques for your paper currency
- Use the paper currency of your country to make payments.

Let's analyse each of the above to see how various entities would settle transactions and transfer money when the paper currency of your country is not available domestically or internationally.

Travellers can transfer money electronically between bank accounts present either within or outside your jurisdiction just as they do today. The foreign-issued debit and credit cards that are acceptable within your country should be allowed to be used just the way they are today after the transition to a paper currency-free economy. When these cards are used to make payments or money is transferred from a bank account present in a foreign jurisdiction to an account in your jurisdiction, the identity of the receiver will be visible, even if the identity of the payer is not.

The foreign paper currency and traveller's cheques that travellers bring with them can be credited to a bank account opened upon their arrival in your country. Such banking facilities should be available at all major airports and other locations throughout the country, just the way you have money changers present at all major airports and at various locations in major cities. The procedure has to be simple and fast, i.e. they produce their passport as proof of their identity, their biometric identity is recorded, a bank account is opened and they are issued with a debit card. Recording and attaching the biometric identity of the account holder to the account will deter any visitors who may want to indulge in unlawful activities as they will be aware that their transactions are visible. The amount of foreign currency they want to exchange is credited into their bank account. Any balance in their bank account is converted into another foreign currency or traveller's cheques when they want it, e.g. when they depart.

The travellers will not be able to bring in the paper currency of your country after you transition to a paper currency-free economy as the process of transition involves recalling it completely, including from overseas territories. They will have to make alternative arrangements to settle transactions and transfer money while they are in your country. Those arrangements have been discussed above, i.e. they can:

- Bring debit or credit cards accepted within your country
- Transfer money electronically between bank accounts
- Bring a foreign currency that can be credited into their bank account
- Bring traveller's cheques that can be credited into their bank accounts.

The next question is what options will your country's residents have when they go abroad? They can exercise the following options:

- Debit cards accepted in foreign jurisdictions
- Credit cards accepted in foreign jurisdictions
- Transfer money electronically between bank accounts
- Traveller's cheques
- Foreign paper currency.

They will be able to buy traveller's cheques or foreign paper currency by making a payment from their bank account electronically.

An active step

The use of paper currency is declining while the use of electronic payments is increasing by the day. In the future, the use of paper currency to make payments will decline even further. But even a small amount of paper currency still being in circulation will prevent a society from becoming free of corruption and professional crime, because entities that want their transactions to remain hidden will use paper currency if they have that option. There would always be enough paper currency for a small percentage of entities to use it for all of their transactions and thus keep their activities hidden; they would be able to conduct their activities, without leaving a visible trail.

Freedom from corruption and professional crime can only be achieved when the use of paper currency within an economy is totally prohibited by law and all transfers of money are made electronically from one bank account to another. It is only then that all transactions between all entities will be visible, and entities intending to indulge or indulging in illegal activities will find it difficult to do so.

3　The technicalities

Partial or complete transition

I have heard the story that when people first saw the steam engine, they did not believe that it could run on tracks of iron. Today watching a train running on tracks of iron does not look like any miracle to us, but it would have been nothing short of a miracle to those who witnessed its first experimental run. Impossible is nothing and nothing is impossible. The transition to a paper currency-free economy can either be complete or partial and most of the countries can either go for a complete transition or a partial one. A complete transition is one where currency notes and coins of all denominations are recalled and people use only electronic means to settle transactions or transfer money. The second path is a partial transition, where currency notes above a certain denomination are recalled and replaced with electronic currency but paper currency notes and coins below that denomination are used alongside electronic options to settle transactions or transfer money. Most of the developing countries and all the developed ones can go for either a partial or a complete transition. The major factors which influence whether you go for complete or partial transition are the level of literacy of residents of your country and the state of the infrastructure needed to support payments via electronic means. Most other factors influencing the transition can be improved within a short span of time.

A partial transition will enable entities that sell goods or services for a low price, e.g. mobile vendors who sell goods worth five dollars or less, to carry on with their trade at a time when they may not be able to use payment terminals or other electronic means. People may not want to use their bank cards to, for example, reward street performers or buy goods from door-to-door vendors initially, so for them small currency notes and coins below a certain denomination can stay in use.

All entities that sell goods and services, whether they operate from a fixed structure or are mobile, can acquire the ability to receive money instantly via electronic means as mobile, wireless payment terminals are available to receive payments with the use of a debit or credit card. For example, we can already pay for a taxi with a debit or credit card. So, there are not really many scenarios where a person would have to use paper currency.

What denominations of the currency notes are kept to make payments after the partial transition is for each government to decide. But what is to be kept in mind is that even a partial transition to a paper currency-free economy can have a big impact on reducing the crime and corruption in your country, so the denomination of the currency notes kept should not be big enough for the corrupt and the criminal to carry on their trade with the only difference being that they now have to carry more currency notes than before. For example, if they used to sell their contraband or illegal services in exchange for two currency notes of a certain denomination, now they sell that for ten currency notes. In that event, all this effort to clean up the community of corruption and crime will be futile. So, the size of the currency note kept has to be big enough for mobile or door-to-door vendors and street performers to sell their goods and entertain people yet small enough for the corrupt and the criminal not to be able to carry on their nefarious business.

In the event that people find it difficult to reward street performers via electronic means, they can be registered and employed by a government to perform just the way they presently do and liven up our streets. Some of us may ask why – the answer is simple: to clean up our streets, our communities and our countries of corruption and crime and making sure at the same time that no one loses his or her job because of a complete transition to a paper currency-free economy.

So, what is the right number of small paper currency notes that should be kept in circulation? That is a decision for a government as it has, or can have, the required information to make that decision. How many small paper currency notes should enter an economy periodically? That again is a decision for each government to make as it has or can have the required information to make that decision. The logic behind a partial transition is to keep smaller currency notes for small purchases and not to fund big purchases with small notes. The policies in existence can be followed. For example, say previously because of a certain level of economic growth and other factors that influenced the monetary policy of a government, 20,000 $10 notes and 10,000 $5 notes would have been printed and entered the economy. If after the partial transition only $5 notes are kept in the paper form, if the level of economic growth and other factors that influence the monetary policy are the same, then

20,000 $10 notes can enter the system electronically and 10,000 $5 notes can enter the system in paper currency form. The logic behind a partial transition is to keep currency notes and coins up to a certain denomination only for minor purchases and not start a system where people start using smaller currency notes but in big numbers.

A country or a monetary union can go for a complete transition if all the entities residing within its jurisdiction can acquire the ability to receive money electronically. The technology and infrastructure present today can allow most countries to undertake a partial transition, but the full benefits will only be realised when there is no paper currency within your economy and the convenience paper currency provides to the corrupt and the criminals will disappear. The process of transition will be easy for developed countries to undertake as they have the required infrastructure to support electronic payments and receipts and the level of literacy is high. Partial transition can continue into full transition when the infrastructure is ready in your country if that is not the case today. The factors that influence whether you go for a partial or complete transition include:

- The state of the infrastructure required to receive and pay money electronically
- The level of literacy in your country
- The availability of payment terminals or other gadgets that allow mobile vendors to receive money electronically into their bank accounts while being mobile
- The ability of your administrative and judicial systems to resolve cases where the payment of money from one entity to another is in dispute.

The infrastructure required to receive and pay money electronically can be improved within a short span of time with some investment, and electronic payment terminals can be made available to mobile vendors so they can receive money electronically while on the go. The level of literacy can be overcome by the quick introduction of letters and numbers to those that need it. They need to know how much money has gone into their bank accounts, what their account balance is and how they can check it. Providing that ability to a person cannot be a hard task. But for countries with a high level of literacy that is not a challenge. Many developed economies can undertake a complete transition to a paper currency-free economy if every mobile vendor has the means, i.e. a wireless payment terminal, to receive money electronically while on the road. Mobile vendors can also use smartphones to sell their merchandise, but in that case the buyer must also have a phone they can use to transfer money to the seller's bank account. The difference a mobile, wireless payment terminal makes is that the buyer will not need to have a smartphone and will be able to use their bank card. The transition to a paper currency-free economy cannot compel people to have mobile phones to make payments; the standard has to be the presence of a payment terminal, either fixed or mobile, with every seller of goods or services and a bank card in the hands of every buyer.

With the bigger currency notes gone, the corrupt, the professional criminals and the sellers of contraband will find it hard to carry on their business. In most parts of the developed world, making payments electronically has become quite common and the majority of vendors accept payments electronically. Those who do not accept payments electronically at present, can acquire the ability to do so.

The corrupt demand bribes and accept kickbacks and professional criminals commit crime and sell contraband because they believe that no one is watching when money moves from one entity to another. When transactions take place electronically where the identities of both the buyer and seller are known, all those who commit crime for money will not do so because they will fear that their transactions will not be hidden and secondly, they could be made to explain their transactions. Even a partial transition should help reduce corruption and crime as currency notes above a certain denomination will be recalled and replaced by electronic currency and smaller currency notes will only be available for minor purchases.

In any economy, be it small or big, the transition to a paper currency-free economy cannot be made overnight. It will require changes to existing laws, it may require additional banking infrastructure and education for citizens about the transition.

The cost of transition

Some banks charge customers monthly fees for maintaining a bank account with them. Let's take the example of a bank that charges five dollars every month as bank fees. So, if you have 1,000 dollars in your account at the start of the year, at the end of the year you will have 940 dollars. Another option you have is to close your bank account and compel your employer to pay you in cash, but that may prove to be very inconvenient for your employer and so they may well decline your request. But at present, you at least have the option because paper currency is in existence and you may not care for your employer's convenience and ask to be paid in cash as opposed to via bank transfer. When paper currency disappears, the option to avoid banks will not be there.

Banks will be very much a part of the system as they are today. But at the end of the day you will want your fifty dollars to be fifty dollars even after ten years and not $49.9999995, just like paper currency today is, irrespective of its purchasing power.

But why should the banks provide a service free of charge? They have their own expenses. You cannot demand that banks provide a fee-free account and yet you do not want to pay any account fee. Who should then make sure that fifty dollars remains fifty dollars, even after twenty years, just like paper currency today does, regardless of the purchasing power? The answer is 'us', or at least our governments, which represent us. If anyone pays it should be the government of a country. Let's delve into why they should do that. It is the government and society that is going to reap the benefits from this transition. The tax revenue of a government may increase manyfold and, depending on the efficiency of its law enforcement agencies, there may be a huge decline in criminal activities. Tax revenues should increase because all business transactions will be visible. The receipts and expenditure of all entities will be visible. Government expenditure will fall because it will not have to print paper currency notes, which will save both money and the trees cut down to make paper for these currency notes. A government will not have to spend money chasing criminals who try to introduce fake currency notes.

The following scenario is just one example of how this can be done. Every entity that resides in or enters a political or economic jurisdiction gets one bank account for which any fees are paid for by the government or where no fee is charged by the bank. This means that every entity has one bank account where the account balance stays at what it is, i.e. $1,000 is $1,000 at the end of any duration unless money is deposited or withdrawn. The government bears all costs towards providing these bank accounts. This can be done in at least two ways: either the government can start its own bank that provides fee-free bank accounts to entities residing and operating within its jurisdiction, or it can enter into agreements with private banks to provide one fee-free bank account to each entity. The guiding principle is that no one has to pay any fee on that account. It is not that all bank accounts have no fee; only one bank account per entity is a fee-free account. The reason for this bank account is that even today you can keep some paper currency in your wallet or at home and you do not have to pay any fees on that. You can keep all of your money at home if the law in your country allows you to. The government of a country can enter into an agreement with all the banks operating within its jurisdiction and give the option to entities residing within its jurisdiction to have one fee-free bank account with any bank. The government may not need to start a new bank, but they could if that proved to be the most economical option.

The same principles apply regarding the provision of electronic payment terminals, which all entities who sell something will need to have. Payment terminals can be provided free to entities whose annual turnover is under a certain amount or the cost of the terminals recovered from them if their tax payable crosses a certain threshold.

In the event of collapse of a bank, a government may guarantee that it will reimburse some amount present in a bank account subject to a ceiling. This compensation must be in addition to what a government might pay as compensation in the event of collapse of a bank before transition to a paper currency free economy, as a new dimension will be added which is the compensation for paper currency which an entity may have kept otherwise.

Factors influencing transition

Any transition to a paper currency-free economy will have to be done by the government of a country. The government will have to take steps to help develop the soft and hard infrastructure needed for this transition. It may need to invest in the development of banking infrastructure, depending on its state within its jurisdiction.

The transition to a paper currency-free economy will be dependent on a few factors in your country; however, getting any of those factors into the necessary state is not unachievable in any part of the world. The following factors may need to be considered.

The banks will form an integral and indispensable part of the system just like today. A transition will not be possible without the presence of a modern banking infrastructure in any country. Parts of the world where the banking infrastructure is well developed and entities use modern banking facilities will find it relatively easy to transition compared with those where the banking infrastructure is not developed and entities do not use modern banking facilities. The banking infrastructure will need to be developed if it is not extensive enough to support the transition, and the transition may take more time in those countries where the banking infrastructure is not well developed. A developed banking sector also implies that a large percentage of the population will not need to be educated about banking.

What will also be advantageous is an entity's ability to access their funds online, although from the point of view of the transition that is purely optional, i.e. only if an entity wants to. If an entity can access their funds online when they want to, that will be advantageous to many and the economy as a whole. Let's take this example: Entity A is in the business of dairy farming. They are located 200 kilometres away from the nearest physical branch of any bank. Entity A sells milk to a company that collects the milk every day. This company transfers the payment to Entity A's bank account electronically. Entity A uses internet banking to pay its suppliers and employees, and does not physically need to go to the bank but is able to receive money and make payments via electronic means.

It cannot be emphasised enough that the transition to a paper currency-free economy is not about having access to or using internet banking, and as such should not be confused with it. Cash sits in the wallets of buyers and in the safes of sellers; in the wallets of buyers it will be replaced by debit cards and in the safes of sellers it will be replaced by electronic payment terminals. That is how simple it is and that is the easiest and most convenient way to become a paper currency-free economy. The use of mobile phones or the internet for the transfer of money is an option but the bottom line has to be debit cards in the hands of buyers and electronic payment terminals in the hands of sellers.

The banking system should be strong enough to be able to stop any attempts to cause any disruption to it. Anyone's ability to interfere with banking data security will have a negative impact on the whole economy. Measures must be in place to keep the data uncorrupted. Without any doubt, our economies are totally dependent on the security of data maintained by the banks even today, so not much will be different in a paper currency-free economy; however, governments may have a more significant role in ensuring that the data maintained by banks is free from corruption and incorruptible.

It is not just the physical but also the intangible supporting infrastructure that will be needed. For example, some laws will need to be amended or introduced to support the transition. The use of cheques may increase because paper currency is not there. So, if disputes in relation to cheques are not resolved quickly, they will have a negative impact on the growth of the economy because the flow of money will slow. Even a single small dispute has an impact, no matter how small it might be. Add all those small ones together and it might give you a figure big enough to have an impact on the whole economy. To explain a bit more, let's say that you sold your goods to an entity who gave you a cheque that was dishonoured. Now you have that much less money to continue your business. Its impact is that your business will buy less. This implies that all the businesses combined within this economy will have that much less money; the purchasing power of businesses will decrease and they will buy less. When the purchasing power of businesses decreases, their consumption will decrease, which will cause production to decrease. A decrease in production means reduced economic activity, which means lower employment and less tax revenue for a government. The difference between a business entity having the money and a non-business entity having the money is that money in the hands of a business has more chance of entering the economic cycle. All disputes relating to money should be resolved as quickly as possible so that the re-entry of money into the economic cycle is quick. This implies that economic disputes, including disputes relating to cheques, will have to be resolved at a fast pace, and so the infrastructure required for this may have to be put in place.

The ability of entities to use modern banking facilities may also need to be developed, and some education may be necessary. There may be many people who are not very familiar with the payment or receipt of money via electronic means in some parts of the world; they will have to be made aware about what is happening and how the transition to a paper currency-free economy is taking place.

The most important factor to be considered is that the transition to a paper currency-free economy should not have any negative impact on economic activity within the country. Prior to transition, all the entities within an economy should have the means and knowledge to make and receive payments electronically. If all the entities within an economy do not have the means and knowledge to make and receive payments electronically, economic activity within that economy will decrease. This is because some entities will not be able to sell what they can offer or buy the goods and services they need.

Ability to open a bank account with a fake identity

The purpose of a transition to a paper currency-free economy will be defeated if any entity, either natural or artificial, is capable of opening a bank account using a fake identity. Attempts to open bank accounts with fake identities may increase substantially when there is no paper currency around. This is because entities that want to hide their activities will try to get bank accounts with fake identities. If that is allowed, the purpose of the transition will be defeated. It must be made sure that banks verify an entity's identity before they are allowed to operate a bank account and that the banks are provided with the required support to be able to do this. On the plus side, directing and monitoring the work of banks that operate within a jurisdiction is much easier than doing the same with the entities that deal with the banks. It is easier to implement the standard required from the start than to clean it up later.

If anyone, be it a natural entity or an entity created by the operation of the law, has the ability to open a bank account with a fake identity, the transition to a paper currency-free economy will not be able to reduce corruption and crime effectively. It is very important that no entity residing or operating within a jurisdiction is capable of opening or operating a bank account under a fake identity.

Those who know me know me by the name of Vikram Vashisht. I can change my name and open a bank account with my new name, and if I want to stay hidden then with a little effort I can get a fake identity and fake supporting documents and open a bank account with that fake identity – and no one may ever know who I really am. It is quite possible that to get fake documents supporting my fake identity I may not need any professional help and just my laptop and printer could give me what I need. But what I would find difficult to change are the unique identities given to us by nature, i.e. the biometric identities such as our fingerprints or iris signatures etc. We can use the technology available to our advantage to make our communities free from corruption. The biometric identity of an account holder can be obtained by a bank and attached to an account holder's accounts to ensure that those who want to open bank accounts using fake identities find it hard to do so. Otherwise, all the corrupt and criminal will open bank accounts with fake identities and be able to do their business as usual, and any transition to a paper currency-free economy to reduce or stop corruption and crime will not have much impact. Attaching the biometric identities of account holders to bank accounts will help reduce crime and corruption because those who would want to have bank accounts under fake identities will not be able to do that.

The software used must have the function to group all bank accounts that have the same biometric identity attached to them.

Preferably, the following details of an account holder must be present on a bank's file:

- Two different forms of biometric identity
- Photograph of the account holder
- Documents supplied by the account holder that establish their identity
- Any other details or formalities required under your banking regulations.

The biometric identities of new account holders can be obtained at the start of operation of their bank account with a bank. The process of obtaining the biometric identities of existing account holders is not a one-day process. It will take time. Entities both natural and artificial will have to be given a time frame to have bank accounts if they do not already have one. Entities whose biometric details are not recorded will have to be given a time frame to have their biometric identities obtained by the banks for them to be able to operate bank accounts after a certain date. Similarly, the biometric identity of the authorised natural person who operates the bank account of an artificial entity must be obtained and recorded by the bank. The process of obtaining a biometric identity should involve a visit to the branch of a bank. To ensure that bank employees do not record fake biometric identities, the identity of the bank employee who records the biometric identity of an account holder must be recorded by the bank. So, the bank knows which of its employees captured and recorded my biometric identity. This needs to be visible only internally; I as a customer of the bank do not need to see this information.

We have seen a surge in the sale of debit cards that you can buy off the shelf. You can get your paper currency credited onto these debit cards. The vendors of these cards ask for nearly no identification about the buyer. All debit cards sold today or after the transition to a paper currency-free economy should be sold only after the identity of the buyer is verified and recorded, i.e. your identity as per the social documents that are required and your biometrics.

Take a look at this scenario to see how someone may try to open a bank account with a fake identity and false biometric data to try and dodge the system. They may send someone else, whose activities they have control over, to a bank to get the account opened, with documents that identify this person as someone else. In this case the biometric identity of the person who is sent to the bank gets recorded with a fake social identity.

After the bank account has been opened using a fake identity and someone else's biometric data, the person who actually operates this bank account does not have his biometric or social identity recorded with the bank. They could use this bank account to receive money from illegal activities because they know that their transactions are not visible because their identity is not attached to that account; the social details are fake and the biometric identity on the bank file is not their biometric identity, so if someone complains or the bank account is monitored by law enforcement authorities, they cannot easily be caught.

Detailed procedures will have to be put into place to stop this fraud. It is not best practice to accept documents supporting identity at face value. The procedures should include the verification of identification documents from the source of their origin and matching the details the bank obtains first hand with the details it obtains from other sources.

Even if someone is able to open and operate a bank account with a fake social identity or false biometric data:

- The movement of money into and out of this bank account will be visible
- All bank accounts attached to this false biometric identity will be visible and so would the movement of money into and out of these accounts
- Spending on the utilities of daily life from these accounts will help track the person whose biometric identity is recorded on the bank file
- The account could be frozen until the required formalities are met.

The details mentioned in this section are very much needed to ensure no corruption and less professional crime. In fact, obtaining an account holder's biometric identity and other details should be easier than the process of issuing a driver's licence: before a driver's licence is issued, a long list of formalities has to be fulfilled by the person who wants to receive the licence, such as proof of identity, proof of residence, a computer test of road rules and regulations and then the practical test of driving on a road. Obtaining the biometric identity and other details as mentioned above should be an easy job compared to issuing a driver's licence. It will ensure that entities will not be able to open bank accounts with fake identities, which will ensure that they cannot demand bribes and kickbacks and will be less likely to engage in professional crime. To achieve a state of no corruption, less crime, economic development and peace, the cost of obtaining and recording the biometric identity of every bank account holder can be funded by the government of a country, if needed.

Those who want to manipulate the system will exploit the smallest gap to keep their transactions hidden, and that smallest gap will give them the required comfort to indulge in corruption and professional crime. It is imperative that all gaps are removed and no room is left for the antisocial entities to manoeuvre, keeping in mind that no measure should have a negative impact on the economic activity within your jurisdiction. In simple words, all the entities that indulge in lawful economic activity should have the means to electronically receive money and make payments at all times.

The speed of processing

The speed of processing transactions electronically should be faster than it is today. In a nutshell, the speed should be at least as fast as the speed of cash transactions. Anything slower than that will need to be improved. Let's take this example, where it takes ten extra seconds when you pay by electronic means. The overall impact of that extra ten seconds multiplied by the number of times entities make transactions gives us the figure that otherwise could have been saved but for the slow processing of transactions. Explaining further, a person who spends ten extra seconds per transaction and shops twice a day spends 7,300 extra seconds a year ($2 \times 10 \times 365$), which is equal to 121 minutes and 40 seconds. So, a country with a shopping population of 20 million, each one of whom spends 20 extra seconds every day, spends 40,555,555 extra hours, which is equal to 1,689,815 days, which could have been spent on anything else but were lost due to the slow processing of the transactions. Let's assume that the per capita hourly domestic production in your country is ten dollars, which is a high figure (the per capita hourly domestic production of a country with a population of twenty-two million and a GDP of $1.6 trillion will be $8.3022, considering that there are twenty-four hours in a day and 365 days in a year). So, the GDP of your country may have risen by $405.55 million if the speed of processing electronic payments had been as fast as the speed with which cash payments are processed.

Development of alternative currencies

The development of alternative currencies will lead to corruption, as corrupt entities may start accepting them to give unlawful favours and do what they should not. Alternative currency can take the form of gifts, gift vouchers or foreign paper currency, amongst others.

The use of foreign paper currency to make payments and settle debt should be prohibited by law, if that is not already the case, because if that is allowed then some entities may start accepting foreign paper currency to carry on their business without leaving any visible trail. Take the example of an entity that wants to keep its transactions hidden, and starts accepting foreign paper currency from another entity. All the entities operating within an economy may start accepting foreign paper currency to keep their transactions unviewable. The end result in this case is that this foreign currency has taken the place of your local currency and the transition to a paper currency-free economy just resulted in the introduction of a foreign currency, sidestepping the benefits of a paper currency-free economy. So, to stop corruption and achieve the results desired from this transition, the use of foreign paper currency for the settlement of debts and payment of accounts should be prohibited by law.

Gift vouchers cannot be allowed to be used to fill the role that paper currency performs today. Gift vouchers have a role and they should be used precisely – and solely – for that role. They should not perform the role that paper currency does once that paper currency has disappeared. To ensure that gift vouchers do not start acting as alternative currency, as some entities may start accepting kickbacks in the form of gift vouchers instead of a transfer of money into their bank accounts for fear of visibility, new laws may need to be implemented to redeem gift vouchers. For example, a corrupt entity may demand a gift voucher and may do the favour after using that gift voucher. A way to ensure that gift vouchers are not used as alternative currency is recording the identity of the entity redeeming the gift voucher. Proof of identity may not be required at the point of sale of the gift voucher because the bank account used to make payment will provide the details of the buyer, provided the gift voucher is identifiable and linked to a buyer.

The gift vouchers or other similar products should be redeemable only at the store where they were intended to be redeemed. The buyer can be asked about this preference at the time of purchase of the gift voucher. If a chain of stores has multiple stores, still a gift voucher should be redeemable only at the store where it was intended to be redeemed because when we present a gift voucher to someone, we have an idea about their preferences, where they live and how far they will have to travel to redeem that gift voucher. What this will do is that a gift voucher will not be treated as paper currency and will not change hands like paper currency does today. Gift vouchers should not be open gift vouchers, i.e. redeemable by anyone and then reimbursed by the entity which sold these in the first place. Imagine if one store or chain of stores sells gift vouchers which can be redeemed at all other stores or chain of stores within your country, then that gift voucher is as good as paper currency and corrupt and criminal entities will start accepting those gift vouchers in return for the poison which they inject into the community.

The gift vouchers should not be convertible into money except when requested by the original buyer. If the gift vouchers are convertible into money at anyone's request, then they will become a great source for the corrupt and the criminals to carry on their trade; they will accept gift vouchers from the buyers of their poison or those who bribe them willingly or unwillingly and then they will go to the store and get the money credited into their bank accounts. This way the trail of the money may not be visible. The only link might be if the details of the gift voucher are connected to the identity or the bank account details of the buyer and the entity that redeemed the gift voucher.

The gift vouchers sold by any entity should not start acting as alternative currency, because it is the purchasing power of a currency note that makes it lucrative. If anything else gives us that power, we are bound to show it equal respect.

Incorporating these simple provisions into the law right from the beginning is easy. It is better to incorporate these provisions from the start rather than wait for something to go wrong and then make a law. It will be easy to implement these provisions because directing stores that sell gift vouchers or other similar products is not difficult. The products sold by them cannot stay undetected for long and if they break the law it will be known in no time.

The use of instruments of banking such as cheques and bank drafts etc. can continue as it is, because the movement of money between the affected bank accounts will be visible.

Whether privately owned online currencies are accepted by your banks or allowed to be traded or used to make payments within your jurisdiction is an issue for your government to decide. Their impact on your economy today or in the future is a matter for your government to deliberate. Their impact on the stability of your economy and on the economic development of your country is for your government to think over and decide, as is their impact on the ability of certain entities to move money internationally, but the logic behind this book is simple: if the movement of money between entities can stay hidden and does not leave a visible trail of who paid whom or who gave money to whom, then the conditions are perfect for corruption, bribery, kickbacks, professional criminals and sellers of contraband. What should never be allowed is the movement of money from one entity to another and from one account to another that does not leave a visible and identifiable trail. Invisibility of movement of money is heaven for the corrupt and the criminal and we will never be able to create corruption- and crime-free societies unless the movement of money is always visible and identifiable.

The legal tender

After transition to a paper currency-free economy, all transfers of money will be via electronic means only, from one bank account to another, and the electronic currency issued by the central bank of your country will replace all domestic paper currency. What gives strength to paper currency is the question that needs to be looked into: why will you sell something in exchange for a piece of paper or polymer? The answer to the strength of electronic currency lies here. Centuries back, when there was no paper currency or coins of metal, bartering was the way to go. You could buy something in exchange for something else. That system certainly made commerce difficult, as at a time when you wanted to eat apples, the seller may not have wanted what you had to offer. The bartering system could never have let an economy achieve its full potential because someone may not have wanted your mangoes when you needed their apples. Coins made of precious metals subsequently came into use and certainly made trade a bit easier. Then some governments introduced paper currency, which was very easy to carry and an absolute boon for commerce. You could sell your produce without the need to buy anything else instantly. You could use paper currency to fulfil your needs at any time of your choice. A government did not have to mine any metal either, though it did have to safeguard its paper currency against counterfeiting.

But what characteristic does paper currency have? Why was it so readily accepted and why is it so readily accepted today? Why is a piece of paper accepted to make payments and settle debt?

Paper currency is a medium that facilitates payments and trade. The supply of paper currency is controlled by a government in order to keep the economy working efficiently. A piece of paper or polymer would not have much value if it were not a currency note. Imagine giving a paper currency note to someone who may never have seen one, or imagine the transition to paper currency. What would people have thought about the notes initially? Why should I take a piece of paper from someone and give him something more real like, let's say, wheat, coffee or fruit? Similarly, the transition to a paper currency-free economy is about facilitating the movement of money in a modern way. The transition will bring with it all the benefits of paper currency plus the visibility.

Coming back to the question as to why a currency note of paper is accepted to settle debt, this is because it is legal tender, issued by the government of that jurisdiction. For example, in Australia a currency note is legal tender throughout Australia and its territories and in the United States a currency note is legal tender for all debts, public and private. The fact that a currency note is legal tender gives value to a small piece of paper. The intrinsic value of a piece of paper or polymer that is called a currency note is not much, and without being legal tender no piece of paper will be enough to settle any debt. On the same count, the figures sitting inside your bank account are not valuable on their own; they are valuable because they represent currency notes, which are legal tender.

For transition from paper currency to electronic currency, every unit of electronic currency issued by a government will have to be made a legal tender by that government, just as every unit of paper currency issued by a government is a legal tender. If the paper currency in your country carries a promise by the government of your country, then the electronic currency also will have to carry the same promise. Electronic currency will have to be protected like paper currency, and no entity except a government should have the authority to issue or cancel any unit of its electronic currency. In a nutshell, electronic currency will have to have all the characteristics paper currency has except the physical appearance.

The electronic currency

A currency note of paper or polymer is a legal tender issued by the government of a country or its agency, such as a central bank or reserve bank. Every paper currency note has a number assigned to it by a central bank, which uniquely identifies it. Units of electronic currency can be numbered and issued by a central bank in just the same way. The numbers should be assigned by the central bank (or any other agency authorised by a government) of a country. Assigning numbers will make sure that fake electronic currency is not introduced and that no one has the ability to increase or decrease the volume of electronic currency except a central bank. This will also help the central bank keep a check on the generation or introduction of fake electronic currency. Introduction of currency without the corresponding growth in production will cause inflation, and secondly, if anyone has the ability to do that except the government of a country or its agencies, they will be in a position to cause harm to that country's economy. By assigning numbers to the electronic currency the risk of that happening will be minimised. The illustrations following this discussion will explain how this can be done.

Every denomination will have to be numbered, from the smallest to the largest. The denominations that do not get used within an economy can be withdrawn by a central bank; for example, if nothing is sold for one cent then in future that one cent denomination can be withdrawn.

Giving numbers to electronic currency will make sure that no entity creates any fake electronic currency, or if it does, it will be detected. Electronic currency can be numbered the same way as paper currency is numbered. Twenty dollars in one bank account do not need to have twenty different numbers. Those twenty dollars can have one number assigned by the central bank. Those twenty dollars should not be able to be divided into any smaller denominations, just the way you cannot cut your $20 note into two to make two separate ten dollar payments. These twenty dollars will travel as twenty dollars forever, with only one number assigned.

Another principle related to this is that the electronic currency unit, i.e. the currency denomination, and the electronic currency number travel as one unit when money travels between banks. When you make a payment of money to someone, the electronic currency denomination keeps its assigned electronic currency number. But, electronic currency units are not attached to any entity's bank account. Your money sitting inside your bank account does not have any electronic currency units assigned to it. This is in keeping with the principle that when you go to a bank today and deposit paper currency into your account, the bank increases your account balance by that amount and it promises to repay you your money, but it does not promise to give you the same physical currency notes that you deposited. The bank does not write your account number on that money and put it into a box with your account number on – it pools it with the other money it receives from other customers. When you withdraw money, it takes money out of its safe, gives it to you and reduces your account balance by that amount.

A question can be asked, why do currency notes stay as legal tender and stores of value in economies on an ongoing basis when we are not exactly sure about how much production there will be in any economy tomorrow? It is because production and consumption are ongoing processes. When you sell your product to someone for currency notes and that person consumes that product, you can buy products that can be bought with those currency notes because production is an ongoing process. The volume of currency notes within an economy can be adjusted if there is an increase or decrease in domestic production or to achieve the desired results of a monetary policy. Similarly, electronic currency units will have all the characteristics of paper currency except the physical appearance.

The electronic currency account

Only the central bank of a country should have the authority to issue electronic currency accounts and to generate, introduce or withdraw electronic currency units. The electronic currency units are generated by the central bank and then transferred to the electronic currency accounts of all other banks. The electronic currency account of a central bank is maintained by the central bank itself, and is used to increase or decrease the volume of electronic currency units.

The rationale, basis and methods for increasing or decreasing the volume of electronic currency, and therefore for the movement of electronic currency units between the electronic currency account of a central bank and other banks, can be the same as they are today.

Let's look at a simple illustration, where the electronic currency account of Bank A has a balance of $493.63. This electronic currency account and the electronic currency units sitting inside it have been issued by a central bank.

This is how the electronic currency account of Bank A will look:

Table 3.1 The electronic currency account of Bank A

Electronic Currency Account	
Currency Denomination	*Electronic Currency Number*
$100	AB1356CD
$100	EG2395BD
$100	CG7925WR
$100	AV2378YU
$50	FG5678GH
$20	GH5678UI
$20	YU5689OP
$2	YO4589GH
$1	YU3478KJ
Cents	
50	C1
10	C2
2	C3
1	C4
$493.63	**Total**

Cents can be written as 0.5, 0.1, 0.02 and 0.01

There are two places this electronic currency account can sit: on the server of a central bank or on the server of the respective bank. The method of verification of the authenticity of electronic currency units will depend on where an electronic currency account sits. The verification requirements will be different if an account is held on the server of a bank compared to when it sits on the server of the central bank that issued the electronic currency. Those methods and requirements have been discussed under a separate heading.

Banks around the world that use a currency issued by a particular central bank will have to apply to that central bank for an electronic currency account. The banks can receive electronic currency units into their electronic currency accounts and transfer the units into other electronic currency accounts to settle their transactions. Electronic currency units can travel only between electronic currency accounts issued by the same central bank.

Now, an account holder makes a payment of $172.12 to another entity that has its bank account with Bank B. Below is an example of the electronic currency units that are randomly transferred by Bank A (currency units can also be selected on the basis of first in, first out) from its electronic currency account to the electronic currency account of Bank B to settle the transaction.

Table 3.2 The electronic currency units transferred from Bank A to Bank B

Currency Denomination	Electronic Currency Number
$100	AB1356CD
$50	FG5678GH
$20	YU5689OP
$2	YO4589GH
Cents	
10	C2
2	C3
$172.12	**Total**

The electronic currency account of Bank A, after the settlement of the above transaction, has a balance of $321.51. Bank A's electronic currency account will look like this:

Table 3.3 The electronic currency account of Bank A after the settlement of the transaction

Electronic Currency Account	
Currency Denomination	Electronic Currency Number
$100	EG2395BD
$100	CG7925WR
$100	AV2378YU
$20	GH5678UI
$1	YU3478KJ
Cents	
50	C1
1	C4
$321.51	**Total**

Customers of banks will not need to have the information regarding the electronic currency units that were transferred between banks to settle their transactions.

Let's look at another illustration: Entity A transfers $100 from its bank account with Bank G to its bank account with Bank C. Bank G transfers five $20 electronic currency units from its electronic currency account to the electronic currency account of Bank C to settle the transaction.

For the purpose of this illustration, the following electronic currency units travel between the electronic currency accounts of the two banks:

Table 3.4 List of electronic currency units that travel between Bank G and Bank C

Electronic Currency Number	Currency Denomination
AB1356CD1	$20
EG2395BD2	$20
CG7925WR3	$20
AV2378YU5	$20
FG5678GH6	$20
Total	**$100**

This is how the balance sheet or the statement of assets and liabilities of Bank C will look after this transaction:

Table 3.5 Balance sheet of Bank C after it has received electronic currency units

Assets	Amount	Liabilities	Amount
Electronic Currency Account	100	Creditor (Entity A)	100
Total	**100**	**Total**	**100**

Entity A has an account balance of $100. The electronic currency units are not attached to Entity A's bank account, rather they sit in the electronic currency account of this bank. The electronic currency account of Bank C will look like this:

Table 3.6 The electronic currency account of Bank C after it has received electronic currency units

Electronic Currency Account

Electronic Currency Number	Currency Denomination
AB1356CD1	$20
EG2395BD2	$20
CG7925WR3	$20
AV2378YU5	$20
FG5678GH6	$20
Total	**$100**

Bank C lends $20 to Entity Y, which makes a payment to ABC Enterprises who have their bank account with Bank T. This is how the balance sheet of Bank C will look after this transaction:

Table 3.7 Balance sheet showing transaction with Entity Y

Assets	Amount	Liabilities	Amount
Electronic Currency Account	80	Creditor (Entity A)	100
Debtor (Entity Y)	20		
Total	**100**	**Total**	**100**

This is how the electronic currency account of Bank C will look after the above transaction:

Table 3.8 The electronic currency account of Bank C after loan to Entity Y

Electronic Currency Number	Currency Denomination
AB1356CD1	$20
EG2395BD2	$20
CG7925WR3	$20
AV2378YU5	$20
Total	**$80**

Assuming that a bank is at liberty to transfer any electronic currency unit it wants to.

This is how the balance sheet of Bank T will look after the transaction:

Table 3.9 The balance sheet of Bank T after receiving electronic currency units

Assets	Amount	Liabilities	Amount
Electronic Currency Account	20	Creditor (ABC Enterprises)	20
Total	**20**	**Total**	**20**

This is how the electronic currency account of Bank T appears after the above transaction:

Table 3.10 The electronic currency account of Bank T after it has received electronic currency units

Electronic Currency Number	Currency Denomination
FG5678GH6	$20
Total	**$20**

We have seen in the above illustrations that when money is transferred to an entity that has a bank account with a different bank, the electronic currency units travel from the electronic currency account of the transferring bank to the electronic currency account of the receiving bank to settle the transaction. It is assumed that both banks have electronic currency accounts issued by the same central bank. If the transferring and receiving banks do not have electronic currency accounts issued by the same central bank, then the transaction cannot be settled by transferring the electronic currency units.

Let's see how the transaction occurs when a payment is made by one entity to another when both have accounts with the same bank. This is the balance sheet of Bank C from the previous example:

Table 3.11 The balance sheet of Bank C

Assets	Amount	Liabilities	Amount
Electronic Currency Account	80	Creditor (Entity A)	100
Debtor (Entity Y)	20		
Total	**100**	**Total**	**100**

Now Entity A makes a payment of $30 to MK Enterprises, who open a bank account with Bank C prior to transfer. This is how the balance sheet will look after the transaction:

Table 3.12 Balance sheet of Bank C after MK Enterprises opens account and receives payment from Entity A

Assets	Amount	Liabilities	Amount
Electronic Currency Account	80	Creditor (Entity A)	70
Debtor (Entity Y)	20	Creditor (MK Enterprises)	30
Total	**100**	**Total**	**100**

As the money has moved between two different bank accounts within the same bank, Bank C's electronic currency account balance does not change at all. So, the bank has all the money it had before. This is what the electronic currency account looks like after the transaction:

Table 3.13 Bank C's electronic currency account after the transaction

Electronic Currency Number	Currency Denomination
AB1356CD1	$20
EG2395BD2	$20
CG7925WR3	$20
AV2378YU5	$20
Total	**$80**

Now, Entity G, a foreign entity, deposits 40 units of foreign currency Y into Bank C. Let's assume that one dollar is equal to one unit of foreign currency Y. This is how the balance sheet of Bank C looks after this transaction:

Table 3.14 The balance sheet of Bank C after deposit of foreign currency

Assets	Amount	Liabilities	Amount
Electronic Currency Account	80	Creditor (Entity A)	70
Foreign Currency Y Account	40	Creditor (MK Enterprises)	30
Debtor (Entity Y)	20	Creditor (Entity G)	40
Total	**140**	**Total**	**140**

Entity G makes a payment of twenty dollars to an entity that has its account with another bank from the bank account it has with Bank C. This is what the balance sheet of Bank C looks like after the transaction:

Table 3.15 Balance sheet of Bank C after payment made by an account holder

Assets	Amount	Liabilities	Amount
Electronic Currency Account	60	Creditor (Entity A)	70
Foreign Currency Y Account	40	Creditor (MK Enterprises)	30
Debtor (Entity Y)	20	Creditor (Entity G)	20
Total	**120**		**120**

The electronic currency account of Bank C after this transaction will look like this:

Table 3.16 The electronic currency account of Bank C after the settlement of Entity G's transaction

Electronic Currency Number	Currency Denomination
AB1356CD1	$20
EG2395BD2	$20
CG7925WR3	$20
Total	**$60**

Let's take another example where Entity A, when leaving the country, gets twenty units of foreign currency Y.

This is how the balance sheet of Bank C will look after the transaction:

Table 3.17 Balance sheet of Bank C after withdrawal of foreign currency by account holder Entity A

Assets	Amount	Liabilities	Amount
Electronic Currency Account	60	Creditor (Entity A)	50
Foreign Currency Y Account	20	Creditor (MK Enterprises)	30
Debtor (Entity Y)	20	Creditor (Entity G)	20
Total	**100**		**100**

Let's take another example, where an entity that does not have an account with this bank demands ten units of foreign currency Y and makes a payment by transferring money from their bank account with another bank.

This is how the balance sheet of Bank C looks after the transaction:

Table 3.18 Balance sheet of Bank C after withdrawal of foreign currency by an entity that does not have an account with the bank

Assets	Amount	Liabilities	Amount
Electronic Currency Account	70	Creditor (Entity A)	50
Foreign Currency Y Account	10	Creditor (MK Enterprises)	30
Debtor (Entity Y)	20	Creditor (Entity G)	20
Total	**100**		**100**

The electronic currency account of Bank C will now have electronic currency units totalling seventy dollars.

The following illustrations show how the system works if you decide to go for a partial transition. In the case of a partial transition, currency notes above a certain denomination are recalled and only those below a certain denomination are kept to be used along with a system of electronic payments. This illustration shows the balance sheet of a bank after a partial transition. For the purpose of this illustration, all currency notes and coins up to five dollars are kept and all currency notes above five dollars have been recalled. Following are the balance sheet, electronic currency account and details of paper currency kept by this bank.

Table 3.19 The balance sheet of a bank after a partial transition

Balance Sheet of a Bank			
Assets	Amount	Liabilities	Amount
Electronic Currency	150	Creditors	200
Cash (paper currency)	50		
Total	**200**	**Total**	**200**

Table 3.20 The electronic currency account of a bank

Electronic Currency Account of this Bank

Electronic Currency Denomination	Electronic Currency Number
$100	ASDF1234
$50	GHJK6789

Table 3.21 The paper currency this bank holds

Cash (Paper Currency) Details of this Bank

Denomination	Quantity	Total
$5	9 notes	45
$1	5 notes	5
Total		**50**

During a business day, the following takes place:

1. An account holder deposits five dollars in cash (paper currency notes) into its bank account
2. An account holder withdraws ten dollars in cash from its bank account
3. An account holder makes a payment of fifty dollars electronically to an entity that has its bank account with another bank.

The above three after these transactions will look like this:

Table 3.22 The balance sheet after the transactions

Balance Sheet of this Bank

Assets	Amount	Liabilities	Amount
Electronic Currency	100	Creditors	145
Cash (paper currency)	45		
Total	**145**	**Total**	**145**

Table 3.23 The electronic currency account after the settlement of transactions

Electronic Currency Account of this Bank

Electronic Currency Denomination	Electronic Currency Number
$100	ASDF1234

Table 3.24 The paper currency this bank holds after the transactions

Cash (Paper Currency) Details of this Bank

Denomination	Quantity	Total
$5	8 notes	40
$1	5 notes	5
Total		**45**

The rolling out of the system

The electronic currency account of a bank that is issued by a central bank can sit on:

- The server of the issuing central bank
- The joint server of two or more issuing central banks
- The server of the respective bank.

The monitoring requirements and the requirements for verification of electronic currency units are different for all the above three categories.

Two or more central banks can also join together and issue electronic currency units and electronic currency accounts and monitor in real time the electronic currency units sitting in the electronic currency accounts of banks. When central banks monitor the electronic currency accounts of banks or verify the authenticity of the electronic currency units issued by them, they are not looking at the business transactions of a bank or a list of its clients – they are only monitoring the electronic currency accounts issued by them and verifying the electronic currency units sitting in those accounts.

In the following illustration, two central banks work together to recall and replace their paper currencies, and in the illustration following that a central bank recalls and replaces paper currency on its own. These two illustrations are shown for understanding as to how the system can be rolled out both individually by a central bank and jointly by two or more central banks.

Let's look at the first illustration:

- Central banks of Countries 1 and 2, Central Bank 1 and Central Bank 2, decide to recall their paper currencies and make a transition to a paper currency-free economy
- The first step they take is to invite applications from interested banks across all jurisdictions for electronic currency accounts,

whether the bank is in Country 1, Country 2 or anywhere else in the world. The criteria for inviting applications may include:
- banks that deal with their currency
- banks that operate in countries with which entities from your country conduct trade or invest
- banks present in countries visited by people from your country

- Country 1 has only one bank B1, Country 2 has only one bank B2 and Country 3 has only one bank B3 (notice here that the central bank of Country 3 has not recalled or replaced its paper currency and is operating the way it was operating before)
- All these three banks apply for electronic currency accounts from Central Bank 1 and Central Bank 2
- These electronic currency accounts can sit either on the servers of Banks B1, B2 or B3, or on the joint server of Central Bank 1 and Central Bank 2
- Whether electronic currency accounts sit on the server of a bank or on the server of a central bank or on the joint server of two or more central banks, the banks can transfer electronic currency units to each other and they can receive electronic currency from each other, but banks cannot see any other bank's electronic currency account, except their own. However, the central banks can monitor all the electronic currency accounts in real time and verify the authenticity of electronic currency units present in them in real time
- Every bank may have an electronic currency account for every juris-diction in which it operates, issued by the central bank of that juris-diction. Bank branches do not have electronic currency accounts. For example, if a bank operates in Country 1 and Country 2, then it may have two electronic currency accounts issued by the Central Bank of Country 1, one for its operations in Country 1 and one for its operations in Country 2
- Only banks, i.e. deposit-taking institutions that are allowed to accept deposits of money, can have electronic currency accounts. Other institutions that do not qualify as a bank or cannot perform all the functions of a bank cannot have electronic currency accounts
- When electronic currency accounts sit on the servers of Banks B1, B2 or B3, the electronic currency units sitting there are verified by Central Bank 1 and Central Bank 2 in real time, and every time they move from one electronic currency account to another, they move through a gateway where their authenticity is verified again. A gateway is a check to ensure that fake electronic currency does not enter an electronic currency account; if there is a fake electronic currency unit, it is detected before it can enter an electronic cur-rency account. A gateway is needed only when electronic currency

accounts sit on the servers of banks. A gateway is not needed when electronic currency accounts sit on the servers of central banks. The central banks will have to ensure in real time that the electronic currency units sitting in electronic currency accounts are authentic

- Banks that operate within your jurisdiction also deal with other currencies, so they will have your electronic currency account and other foreign currency accounts.

The following are the balance sheets of Banks B1, B2 and B3 before the transition:

Table 3.25 The balance sheet of Bank B1 with paper currencies issued by three central banks

Balance Sheet of Bank B1

Assets	Amount	Liabilities	Amount
PCC1	500	Equity	1,500
PCC2	500		
PCC3	500		
TOTAL	**1,500**	**TOTAL**	**1,500**

Table 3.26 The balance sheet of Bank B2 with three different paper currencies

Balance Sheet of Bank B2

Assets	Amount	Liabilities	Amount
PCC1	1,000	Equity	3,000
PCC2	1,000		
PCC3	1,000		
TOTAL	**3,000**	**TOTAL**	**3,000**

Table 3.27 The balance sheet of Bank B3 with three different paper currencies

Balance Sheet of Bank B3

Assets	Amount	Liabilities	Amount
PCC1	2,000	Equity	6,000
PCC2	2,000		
PCC3	2,000		
TOTAL	**6,000**	**TOTAL**	**6,000**

PCC1 is the paper currency issued by Central Bank 1
PCC2 is the paper currency issued by Central Bank 2
PCC3 is the paper currency issued by Central Bank 3

After recalling PCC1 and PCC2 and replacing them with the electronic currencies issued by Central Bank 1 and Central Bank 2 respectively, the electronic currency accounts of Banks B1, B2 and B3 will look like this:

Table 3.28 The electronic currency account of Bank B1 after two of the three paper currencies have been replaced with electronic currency

Electronic Currency Account of Bank B1

Currency	C1, C2
Electronic Currency Number	Denomination
C1A1	500
C2A1	500
TOTAL	**1,000**

Table 3.29 The electronic currency account of Bank B2 after two of the three paper currencies have been replaced with electronic currency

Electronic Currency Account of Bank B2

Currency	C1, C2
Electronic Currency Number	*Denomination*
C1A2	500
C1A3	500
C2A2	500
C2A3	500
TOTAL	**2,000**

Table 3.30 The electronic currency account of Bank B3 after two of the three paper currencies have been replaced with electronic currency

Electronic Currency Account of Bank B3	
Currency	C1, C2
Electronic Currency Number	Denomination
C1A4	500
C1A5	500
C1A6	500
C1A7	500
C2A4	500
C2A5	500
C2A6	500
C2A7	500
TOTAL	**4,000**

The electronic currency units issued by Central Bank 1 start with C1 and the electronic currency units issued by Central Bank 2 start with C2.

Once the system is in operation, Central Bank 1 and Central Bank 2 can see how many electronic currency units issued by them are sitting in the electronic currency account of a particular bank, or in which country, or in which economic jurisdiction and what impact it will have on their economy and the regional and global economy. The questions asked these days, such as about the presence of billions of dollars sitting in foreign, secretive jurisdictions without anyone knowing where it is, will cease to exist and the central banks will have complete knowledge of where the currency issued by them is sitting. If central banks whose currencies are widely accepted share that information, then its impact on global trends in the future will be clear. Money will not sit idle inside banks located in secrecy jurisdictions. Even if a bank is present in a secretive jurisdiction, the electronic currency account of that bank, issued by a central bank, will be visible to that central bank. It is in the interest of a government and a central bank to be able to see how much of the currency issued by the central bank is sitting with a particular bank or in a particular jurisdiction, and what its impact could be when it is used to buy production either from your jurisdiction or somewhere else this currency is accepted. Knowledge regarding how much currency is present in which jurisdiction will help to protect against any effects arising out of unexpected movement of this currency.

You can see above that the electronic currency units do not repeat. The currency units present in one electronic currency account are not present in any other electronic currency account. Central Bank 1 and Central Bank 2 perform checks in real time that there is no electronic currency unit in any electronic currency account that is not issued by them, and also that every currency unit has the denomination and currency number with which it was issued and that no electronic currency unit is present in more than one place.

The balance sheets of Banks B1, B2 and B3 now look like this:

Table 3.31 The balance sheet of Bank B1 after two of the three currencies have been replaced with electronic currency

Balance Sheet of Bank B1

Assets	Amount	Liabilities	Amount
ECC1	500	Capital	1,500
ECC2	500		
PCC3	500		
TOTAL	**1,500**	**TOTAL**	**1,500**

Table 3.32 The balance sheet of Bank B2 after two of the three currencies have been replaced with electronic currency

Balance Sheet of Bank B2

Assets	Amount	Liabilities	Amount
ECC1	1,000	Capital	3,000
ECC2	1,000		
PCC3	1,000		
TOTAL	**3,000**	**TOTAL**	**3,000**

Table 3.33 The balance sheet of Bank B3 after two of the three currencies have been replaced with electronic currency

Balance Sheet of Bank B3

Assets	Amount	Liabilities	Amount
ECC1	2,000	Capital	6,000
ECC2	2,000		
PCC3	2,000		
TOTAL	**6,000**	**TOTAL**	**6,000**

- Here the paper currency issued by Central Bank 1 and Central Bank 2 has been replaced with electronic currency that is present in the electronic currency accounts of these three banks
- The three banks still have the paper currency issued by Central Bank 3, the central bank of Country 3
- Central Bank 3 has not made the transition to replace its paper currency with electronic currency
- Central Bank 3 can issue electronic currency accounts to banks it wants to, either on its own or it can join Central Bank 1 and Central Bank 2
- Central Bank 3 decides not to join Central Bank 1 and Central Bank 2
- Central Bank 3 decides to replace its paper currency PCC3 with electronic currency ECC3 and invites applications for electronic currency accounts from banks. Banks B1, B2 and B3 apply.

The electronic currency accounts of Banks B1, B2 and B3 as issued by Central Bank 3 will look like this after the recalling and replacement of paper currency with electronic currency units:

Table 3.34 The electronic currency account of Bank B1 after the third paper currency is replaced with electronic currency

Electronic Currency Account of Bank B1	
Currency	C3
Electronic currency number	Denomination
C3A1	500
TOTAL	**500**

Table 3.35 The electronic currency account of Bank B2 after the third paper currency is replaced with electronic currency

Electronic Currency Account of Bank B2	
Currency	C3
Electronic currency number	Denomination
C3A2	500
C3A3	500
TOTAL	**1,000**

Table 3.36 The electronic currency account of Bank B3 after the third paper currency is replaced with electronic currency

Electronic Currency Account of Bank B3	
Currency	C3
Electronic currency number	Denomination
C3A4	500
C3A5	500
C3A6	500
C3A7	500
TOTAL	**2,000**

PCC3, i.e. the paper currency of Country 3, has been recalled and replaced by Central Bank 3 with ECC3, the electronic currency of Country 3.

An electronic currency account can sit on the server of the central bank that issued it. This is much easier than the other option, where the electronic currency accounts sit on the servers of banks, in which case much stronger monitoring methods and gateways will be required to ensure that fake electronic currency is not generated; when the electronic currency accounts sit on the server of a central bank, monitoring them will be much easier. Banks can receive electronic currency units issued by a central bank and send them to other banks but they cannot generate electronic currency units.

There are about 15,000 banks globally and approximately 180 United Nations recognised currencies, so each of these 15,000 banks may have 180 electronic currency accounts when all the central banks have replaced their paper currency with electronic currency, and each of these 180 central banks may have 15,000 electronic currency accounts. Let's say that a bank in Chile and a bank in Vietnam want to settle their accounts in pounds sterling: they do so by transferring money between electronic currency accounts issued to them by the Bank of England, which may sit on the server of the Bank of England.

The rolling out of the system – cont'd

A bank is a deposit-taking institution, an institution that can accept deposits of money, grant loans and which is allowed by the central bank of a country to operate as a bank. It is only the banks that are issued an electronic currency account and not the branches of those banks. So, if there are ten banks within your jurisdiction and they have 100 branches, then your central bank issues ten electronic currency accounts within your jurisdiction. Issuing an electronic currency account to every branch will serve no additional purpose and will only make the process of regulating and monitoring electronic currency accounts cumbersome.

Now let's say that one of these ten banks operates in another economic jurisdiction or another country; for that second economic jurisdiction or country, that bank may have another electronic currency account issued by your central bank. This will be needed for the bank to ascertain the viability of its operations inside and outside of that country. The banks can transfer electronic currency units between these electronic currency accounts. This is more practical than giving one electronic currency account to a bank for all economic jurisdictions or for all countries. It will also let a central bank monitor the use and presence of its currency across various jurisdictions. For example, if Bank A operates only in Australia and Canada, then the Reserve Bank of Australia issues Bank A two electronic currency accounts, one for its operations in Australia and one for its operations in Canada. Bank A can transfer electronic currency units between its two electronic currency accounts.

Illustration: Bank A has three branches, 1, 2 and 3. Their balance sheets before transition to a paper currency-free economy look like this:

Table 3.37 Balance sheet of Branch 1 of Bank A showing cash as an asset

Balance Sheet of Branch 1 of Bank A

Assets	Amount	Liabilities	Amount
Cash	100	Equity	200
Debtors	700	Creditors	600
Total	**800**	**Total**	**800**

Table 3.38 Balance sheet of Branch 2 of Bank A showing cash as an asset

Balance Sheet of Branch 2 of Bank A

Assets	Amount	Liabilities	Amount
Cash	500	Equity	200
Debtors	300	Creditors	600
Total	**800**	**Total**	**800**

Table 3.39 Balance sheet of Branch 3 of Bank A showing cash as an asset

Balance Sheet of Branch 3 of Bank A

Assets	Amount	Liabilities	Amount
Cash	700	Equity	200
Debtors	100	Creditors	600
Total	**800**	**Total**	**800**

After the transition the balance sheets of the three branches look like this:

Table 3.40 Balance sheet of Branch 1 of Bank A showing electronic currency as an asset

Balance Sheet of Branch 1

Assets	Amount	Liabilities	Amount
Electronic Currency	100	Equity	200
Debtors	700	Creditors	600
Total	**800**	**Total**	**800**

Table 3.41 Balance sheet of Branch 2 of Bank A showing electronic currency as an asset

Balance Sheet of Branch 2

Assets	Amount	Liabilities	Amount
Electronic Currency	500	Equity	200
Debtors	300	Creditors	600
Total	**800**	**Total**	**800**

Table 3.42 Balance sheet of Branch 3 of Bank A showing electronic currency as an asset

Balance Sheet of Branch 3

Assets	Amount	Liabilities	Amount
Electronic Currency	700	Equity	200
Debtors	100	Creditors	600
Total	**800**	**Total**	**800**

The electronic currency account of Bank A (and not of its branches) is as follows:

Table 3.43 The electronic currency account of Bank A

Electronic Currency Account of Bank A	
Electronic Currency Number	*Denomination*
AS1	100
AS2	100
AS3	100
AS4	100
AS5	100
AS6	100
AS7	100
AS8	100
AS9	100
AS10	100
AS11	100
AS12	100
AS13	100

You can see that before the transition, this bank had 1,300 units of cash and after transition this bank has 1,300 units of electronic currency, which is present in its electronic currency account. The electronic currency units can be issued in any denomination, as deemed suitable by a central bank; however, for ease of understanding the electronic currency units for the above illustration have the denomination of 100.

Why does a central bank need the ability to monitor the electronic currency accounts of banks in real time?

It is because a central bank is responsible for maintaining the volume of money within its economic jurisdiction at a certain level. By issuing electronic currency accounts and the electronic currency units present in those accounts, a central bank is allowing a bank to use the electronic currency issued by it. If a bank cannot use a particular currency, then it cannot trade with that currency and thus cannot exist as a bank of that currency. The more currencies a bank has, or the more electronic currencies a bank has or it can receive and provide to its customers as the case may be in the future, the more business it can do and the more profitable it can be.

Secondly, the banks will be confident that the electronic currency units sitting in their electronic currency accounts are not fake. A central bank is only verifying the authenticity of the electronic currency units sitting in an electronic currency account issued by itself, and not in an electronic currency account issued by any other central bank. A bank may have 180 electronic currency accounts; the electronic currency units present in those accounts are verified by their respective central banks. A central bank will be in a position to see how much of the electronic currency it has issued is present in which bank's electronic currency account, even if that bank is 5,000 miles away in another jurisdiction.

Electronic currency accounts should not be issued without the respective central bank having the ability to monitor and verify them in real time. This would only cause chaos.

The ability to monitor electronic currency accounts will give central banks an added advantage when formulating their monetary policies because they will be able to see how much currency they have in circulation in which part of the world and what impact it will have on their proposed actions.

The system will gain strength as central banks whose currencies are widely accepted around the world make the transition and convert their paper currency into electronic currency. The banks that do not have an electronic currency account of a particular central bank will be at a disadvantage because they may not be able to meet the demands of their customers.

How is the authenticity of electronic currency verified?

If paper currency can be counterfeited, so could electronic currency be. Perhaps it could be even easier to introduce fake electronic currency. To protect its economy, the central bank of a country will have to safeguard the electronic currency just as it protects the paper currency, and ensure that fake electronic currency is not introduced into the system; this would have the same impact that the introduction of fake paper currency does. Only the central bank of a country should have the authority to introduce or withdraw electronic currency units.

How the verification of electronic currency is done depends on where the electronic currency account issued by a central bank is being held. As previously discussed, an electronic currency account can sit on:

- The server of a bank
- The server of a central bank
- The joint server of two or more central banks.

When an electronic currency account is sitting on the server of a bank, a central bank must verify in real time that the electronic currency units present in that account are authentic, by matching the electronic currency units present in that account with the record of electronic currency units it has issued and maintains. A central bank must also verify that no electronic currency unit is sitting in more than one place. This is important because if this function is not added then it will not report anything as inauthentic; someone might take advantage of that and create electronic currency units with the same numbers and denominations as originally issued, authentic electronic currency units. Any electronic currency number or denomination that does not match with the records maintained by a central bank or is present in more than one place should be investigated.

The authenticity of electronic currency can also be verified when it moves between electronic currency accounts. For example, Entity A has a bank account with Bank J and makes a payment to Entity B, which has a bank account with Bank K. When this transaction takes place, the electronic currency units will move between two separate electronic currency accounts held at two separate banks. This is the time when the authenticity of electronic currency can be verified by making it enter a gateway. A gateway is a second check.

The two methods discussed above can be combined for extra security. The first method is checking the electronic currency units sitting in the electronic currency account of a bank against the record of electronic currency units maintained by the central bank. The second is when electronic currency units move between the electronic currency accounts of two different banks. It is better to perform checks at both levels because fake electronic currency units may be generated and kept within an organisation if the internal records are not verified, and only genuine electronic currency units may be sent outside while transacting. The second check will detect any fake electronic currency units before they enter an electronic currency account.

The transaction details between entities may be recorded as per the current legal requirements, but the movement of the electronic currency units may be recorded only for the last transaction, especially when the authenticity of the electronic currency units is verified every time it moves between banks. The depth of the records of movement of electronic currency units maintained will be determined by the ability of the systems to detect the fake electronic currency units and of a central bank to investigate.

Let's look at the following example to understand this. Entity A transfers twenty dollars from its bank account with Bank T to its bank account with Bank L. In order to settle the transaction, Bank T transfers an electronic currency unit that has a denomination of $20 and an electronic currency number of 'AB3456DF3' from its electronic currency account to the electronic currency account of Bank L. Now Banks T and L will maintain the record of movement of twenty dollars and the details of the bank accounts involved, as per the current legal requirements, but for how long should Banks T and L maintain the record that an electronic currency unit with currency number 'AB3456DF3' and a denomination of $20 was transferred from Bank T's electronic currency account to Bank L's account? How much detail it includes and for how long this record is to be kept is a question to be answered by a central bank. The presence of these records would help to identify how, if any, fake electronic currency was introduced.

Recalling and replacement of paper currency – the most important factor for transition

The recalling and replacement of paper currency is the most important factor for transition to a paper currency-free economy because paper currency exists at present and the transition is from what exists at present to a future where there is no paper currency. You are leaving the past behind, but you are still building your future on it: the future calculations cannot exist without taking the present into account. If you do not factor the present into your calculations then you cannot build an accurate future. The future, in this case, has to be as accurate a depiction of the present as it can be, otherwise the future will not be the true representation of its base, the base being the present.

In order to maintain a certain level of growth, to keep inflation in check and further their monetary policies, central banks maintain the volume of paper currency within their economic jurisdictions at a certain level. It is that paper currency that is recalled and replaced with electronic currency, so the volume of currency previously issued stays the same.

The volume of electronic currency, i.e. the electronic currency units issued by a central bank, can be increased or decreased as desired by a central bank just the way it does today with paper currency, the difference being that now the electronic currency units will move between its electronic currency account and the electronic currency accounts of banks, to achieve the result desired by the central bank. The electronic currency account of a central bank is not present with any bank but is maintained by the central bank itself.

The system starts working from the day when banks stop accepting and giving paper currency notes, be this all of them or only those above a certain denomination. But before this happens the paper currency present within and outside your economic jurisdiction will have to be recalled and replaced with electronic currency units by a certain date. All the entities present within your economic jurisdiction and the ones outside your jurisdiction who might have your paper currency are to be invited to deposit the recalled paper currency they have and receive a credit in their bank accounts for the amount deposited. There must be a specified date by which all the entities that reside within a jurisdiction are required to deposit the recalled paper currency notes and receive a credit for the amount deposited. After that date, the banks should not accept any paper currency notes; the paper currency notes should lose their status as legal tender to satisfy any debt and should be nothing more than a piece of paper. This information must be conveyed to all entities, whether natural or created by law around the world.

The first impact of this will be that all the 'black money' will start surfacing because entities that might have black money in the form of paper currency will be forced to deposit it into their bank accounts. Even if currency notes under a certain denomination are kept, all notes can be recalled and replaced with newer notes that have new features to ensure that there is no black money in the economy. The status of legal tender to satisfy a debt can be withdrawn from previously issued currency notes after the specified date.

The process of recalling your paper currency present in foreign hands will be similar. All those who have your paper currency or deal with your paper currency will have to be made aware to deposit it into their local banks that accept foreign exchange and get a credit into their bank accounts for the value of the amount deposited. Those currency notes can then be collected from foreign banks by your banks or your central bank and the transactions can be settled:

- Using the existing means
- By replacing your paper currency with electronic currency in the electronic currency account issued by your central bank
- By exchanging paper currency presently in circulation with paper currency notes of larger denominations available after the transition as discussed under a separate heading.

After the date as decided by your government, the currency notes recalled should lose their legal status to satisfy debt both within and outside your economic jurisdiction. Banks both within and outside your jurisdiction should be instructed not to accept your paper currency notes after that specified date.

A central bank will also need to have an electronic currency account of its own and replace all the paper currency it may have kept as reserves with the electronic currency units in that electronic currency account. So, the paper currency held by a central bank is replaced by electronic currency units in its own electronic currency account. This is the electronic currency account where new electronic currency units are generated by a central bank. When a central bank increases the money supply, electronic currency units are transferred from this account to the electronic currency accounts of banks. When a central bank decreases the money supply, electronic currency units move from the electronic currency accounts of banks to the electronic currency account of the central bank.

A central bank can invite applications from all banks around the world who may want to have one of its electronic currency accounts. After the specified date mentioned by the central bank, no paper currency should be replaced with electronic currency; however, an electronic currency account may be issued to a bank at any time.

All banks that use your currency may be invited to apply for your electronic currency account. Banks that do not need your electronic currency account there and then can apply for one in the future, but the banks that apply for your electronic currency account can return your paper currency and have it replaced with your electronic currency units in their electronic currency accounts before the date specified by your central bank. After the specified date, no more paper currency will be replaced by electronic currency units by the central bank. This date is important to the process being completed within a stipulated time frame.

Recalling and replacement procedure – cont'd 1

Paper currency can be replaced with electronic currency when the process of recalling is in progress either on a day-to-day or other periodic basis. The paper currency collected by the banks is returned to the central bank and the central bank replaces it with electronic currency.

The following illustration shows the balance sheet of a bank at the start of 'day 1', where electronic currency has not come into existence and there is no electronic currency account.

Table 3.44 Balance sheet of a bank before recalling and replacement of paper currency

Assets	Amount	Liabilities	Amount
Cash (paper currency)	100	Creditor (depositor)	100

During 'day 1' a depositor deposits 100 units of local paper currency. 'Day 1' is the day when the recalling and replacement of paper currency starts. Let's assume that the replacement of paper currency with electronic currency occurs at 11pm daily. This is how the balance sheet of this bank will look at 10.59pm.

Table 3.45 Balance sheet of a bank after deposit of cash before recalling of paper currency

Assets	Amount	Liabilities	Amount
Cash (paper currency)	200	Creditor (depositor)	200

The replacement takes place at 11pm. This example assumes that there is a mechanism in place between the central bank and this bank regarding how much paper currency it wants to replace that day and how the central bank is going to collect the recalled paper currency. Such an arrangement will have to be in place to replace the paper currency with electronic currency. This is how the balance sheet of this bank looks after the paper currency has been replaced with electronic currency at 11pm.

Table 3.46 Balance sheet of a bank after recalling and replacement of paper currency with electronic currency

Assets	Amount	Liabilities	Amount
Local Electronic Currency	200	Creditor (depositor)	200
Cash (paper currency)	0		
Total	**200**	**Total**	**200**

Now after the replacement, this bank has an electronic currency account. It can be agreed between this bank and the central bank as to what denominations of electronic currency units it requires, and the bigger denominations can be exchanged for smaller ones as required. The electronic currency account of this bank may look like this:

Table 3.47 Electronic currency account of a bank after its paper currency has been recalled and replaced with electronic currency

Electronic Currency Number	Denomination
ASDF1234	100
ASDF1235	50
ASDF1236	20
ASDF1237	20
ASDF1238	10
Total	**200**

Recalling and replacement procedure – cont'd 2

It is very important that only the paper currency a bank actually physically has and not the promises between banks are replaced with electronic currency, because those promises are based on paper currency; when paper currency is replaced with electronic currency, the banks can settle their accounts as per their agreements and arrangements by transferring electronic currency units between their electronic currency accounts. This will also ensure that the volume of electronic currency will not be more than the volume of paper currency that was in existence before the transition.

Let's look at the following illustration. There are two banks, Bank A in Country 1 and Bank B in Country 2. Their balance sheets are as follows:

Table 3.48 Balance sheet of Bank A

Balance Sheet of Bank A in Country 1

Assets	Amount	Liabilities	Amount
Cash (currency of Country 1)	500	Creditor A	500
Total	**500**	**Total**	**500**

Table 3.49 Balance sheet of Bank B

Balance Sheet of Bank B in Country 2

Assets	Amount	Liabilities	Amount
Cash (currency of Country 2)	500	Creditor B	500
Total	**500**	**Total**	**500**

Creditor A transfers 100 units of currency 1 to Creditor B's bank account in Country 2 (assuming that both currencies have the same value). Their balance sheets after the transaction look like this (assuming that the transaction has not been settled between the two banks as of yet):

Table 3.50 Balance sheet of Bank A after an account holder transfers money to an entity that has an account with Bank B

Balance Sheet of Bank A in Country 1

Assets	Amount	Liabilities	Amount
Cash (currency of Country 1)	500	Creditor A	400
		Bank B	100
Total	**500**	**Total**	**500**

Table 3.51 Balance sheet of Bank B after a foreign entity has transferred money into the bank account of its account holder

Balance Sheet of Bank B in Country 2

Assets	Amount	Liabilities	Amount
Cash (currency of Country 2)	500	Creditor B	600
Bank A	100		
Total	**600**	**Total**	**600**

Here we can see that Bank A owes Bank B 100 units of Currency 1 but there has not been any movement of cash between the two banks.

The central bank of Country 1 invites applications for electronic currency accounts and both banks apply. The central bank of Country 1 issues electronic currency accounts to both banks. Here, paper currency is replaced with electronic currency, since paper currency was the original legal tender. The promises the banks have made to each other are not included. After the banks have the electronic currency accounts, they can settle their accounts with each other simply by transferring the electronic currency units between their electronic currency accounts.

The electronic currency accounts of the two banks look like this:

Table 3.52 Electronic currency account of Bank A before settlement of transaction

Electronic Currency Account of Bank A in Country 1

Electronic Currency Number	Denomination
A1	100
A2	100
A3	100
A4	100
A5	100
Total	**500**

Table 3.53 Electronic currency account of Bank B before settlement of transaction

Electronic Currency Account of Bank B in Country 2

Electronic Currency Number	Denomination
NIL	NIL
TOTAL	**NIL**

Now Bank A transfers 100 units of the electronic currency of Country 1 to Bank B in line with its promise. The electronic currency accounts of Bank A and Bank B will look like this:

Table 3.54 Electronic currency account of Bank A after it has settled the transaction by transferring electronic currency units

Electronic Currency Account of Bank A in Country 1

Electronic Currency Number	*Denomination*
A2	100
A3	100
A4	100
A5	100
Total	**400**

Table 3.55 Electronic currency account of Bank B after it has received electronic currency units as settlement of a transaction

Electronic Currency Account of Bank B in Country 2

Electronic Currency Number	*Denomination*
A1	100
TOTAL	**100**

The balance sheets of the two banks will look like this:

Table 3.56 Balance sheet of Bank A after settlement of a transaction

Balance Sheet of Bank A in Country 1

Assets	*Amount*	*Liabilities*	*Amount*
Electronic Currency (Country 1)	400	Creditor A	400
Total	**400**	**Total**	**400**

Table 3.57 Balance sheet of Bank B after it has received electronic currency into its electronic currency account

Balance Sheet of Bank B in Country 2

Assets	*Amount*	*Liabilities*	*Amount*
Cash (currency of Country 2)	500	Creditor B	600
Electronic Currency (Country 1)	100		
Total	**600**	**Total**	**600**

In the illustration above, we see that the two banks were given electronic currency accounts and afterwards Bank A transfers 100 units of Currency 1 to Bank B's electronic currency account. Now the central bank of Country 1 can see that 100 units of its currency were transferred by Bank A to Bank B; previously it could not see any of the transactions between the two. The kind of questions that arise today about a country's money being present in some other country or some secrecy haven will cease to exist. All electronic currency accounts may sit on this central bank's server, and the banks can receive and send money to other electronic currency accounts issued by this central bank. So, when major currencies transition, the ability of entities to keep money in secrecy jurisdictions will be substantially reduced, and it will be good for the global economy if the central banks that issue major currencies exchange such information with each other.

A second point that needs mentioning is that when a currency is recalled then it will also be recalled from banks present in foreign jurisdictions. This will provide vital information if paper currency was smuggled out of your country. The entities that deposit currency above a certain amount must be asked questions about how that currency came into their possession. Not asking these questions will only legitimise your currency present in their hands if they obtained it through unlawful means. Some criminal entities might try to deposit large amounts of foreign exchange by depositing small amounts through a large number of depositors. So, the first step can be to flag those bank accounts where small deposits of foreign currency are made and then to monitor the flow of money from those bank accounts to the destination bank account. What further measures your government or your central bank put into place to investigate the previously smuggled paper currency and to catch those smugglers lies within their sphere of action.

The fake currency should not be replaced with electronic currency units and as such only genuine currency issued by your central bank should be replaced after verification. There are many currencies in the world that are counterfeited by criminal organisations, mostly outside the jurisdiction of the respective country whose currency they are counterfeiting. Such criminal organisations should not have the opportunity to get their counterfeit currency converted into credit in their bank accounts.

Now let's look at another illustration, the purpose of which is to show that the procedure outlined does not make sense. In this illustration both the paper currency present within a bank and the promises it has made are replaced with electronic currency. The following are the balance sheets of Banks A and B from the illustration discussed previously.

Table 3.58 Balance sheet of Bank A

Balance Sheet of Bank A in Country 1

Assets	Amount	Liabilities	Amount
Cash (currency of Country 1)	500	Creditor A	400
		Bank B	100
Total	**500**	**Total**	**500**

Table 3.59 Balance sheet of Bank B

Balance Sheet of Bank B in Country 2

Assets	Amount	Liabilities	Amount
Cash (currency of Country 2)	500	Creditor B	600
Bank A	100		
Total	**600**	**Total**	**600**

Here you can see that Bank A owes Bank B 100 units of Currency 1. Previously, only the paper currency was replaced with electronic currency. Now, just to show that this does not make any sense, we will replace both the promise and the paper currency. So, the balance sheets of the two banks after the replacements of promises and paper currency of Country 1 with electronic currency of Country 1 will look like this:

Table 3.60 Balance sheet of Bank A after transition to electronic currency

Balance Sheet of Bank A in Country 1

Assets	Amount	Liabilities	Amount
Electronic Currency (Country 1)	500	Creditor A	400
		Bank B	100
Total	**500**	**Total**	**500**

Table 3.61 Balance sheet of Bank B after transition to electronic currency

Balance Sheet of Bank B in Country 2

Assets	Amount	Liabilities	Amount
Cash (currency of Country 2)	500	Creditor B	600
Electronic Currency (Country 1)	100		
Total	**600**	**Total**	**600**

You can see on the face of this that replacing both paper currency and promises between banks does not make sense, because:

1.   Bank A still owes Bank B, 100 units of Currency 1, although the promise by Bank A to Bank B has been converted to electronic currency units by the central bank of Country 1. And even if Bank B frees Bank A of its obligation, the question is why has this central bank acted to free Bank A of its obligation to Bank B?
2.   Secondly, the amount of paper currency issued by the central bank of Country 1 was 500 units, which has now gone up by 100 units without any regard to the level of economic growth that took place over the period of transition to electronic currency. This will result in oversupply of money, which will cause inflation and other negative trends.

So, the right approach is that only the paper currency actually present within the banks is recalled and replaced with electronic currency in their electronic currency accounts. The banks can then settle their debt as per the agreements between them by transferring electronic currency units between their electronic currency accounts.

Recalling and replacement procedure – cont'd 3

The following illustration must be taken into consideration when the recalling and replacement of paper currency with electronic currency takes place.

Table 3.62 Showing recalling and replacement

Bank	Had	Lent	Remaining
1	100	95	5
2	95	90	5
3	90	80	10
4	80	75	5
5	75	65	10
6	65	63	2
7	63	60	3
8	60	57	3
9	57	50	7
10	50	45	5
11	45	0	45
Total	**780**	**680**	**100**

In the above scenario, Bank 1 had 100 dollars and it lent ninety-five dollars to Bank 2, Bank 2 had ninety-five dollars and it lent ninety dollars to Bank 3 and so on. Bank 11 borrowed forty-five dollars from Bank 10; it has not lent any money to anyone and has forty-five dollars.

When recalling and replacement takes place, it is the paper currency present in physical form with these banks that is replaced with electronic currency units in their electronic currency accounts. If you see, the total of the third column is 100, which is the same as the starting point of 100. So, Bank 11 deposits forty-five dollars with the central bank and forty-five dollars in electronic currency units are transferred to its electronic currency account by the central bank, Bank 10 deposits five dollars with the central bank in paper currency and five dollars in electronic currency units are transferred to its electronic currency account by the central bank and so on. The banks can settle their accounts by transferring electronic currency units between their electronic currency accounts.

Recalling and replacement procedure – cont'd 4

The following scenario may or may not arise when recalling and replacement takes place.

If there is a dispute between two banks that Bank 1 requested Bank 2 to pay more money to an entity than it had, for example Bank 1 requested Bank 2 to pay 100 dollars to an entity at a time when Bank 1 had only fifty dollars, then when recalling and replacement takes place, Bank 1's fifty dollars in paper currency will be replaced by fifty dollars in electronic currency units in its electronic currency account; however, to settle its debt with Bank 2 it will need to transfer 100 dollars in electronic currency units to the electronic currency account of Bank 2, but will only have fifty dollars in its electronic currency account. So, Bank 1 owes Bank 2 100 dollars and it has only fifty dollars, so there is a dispute as Bank 1 had requested Bank 2 to transfer more money to an entity than it could request.

This dispute is to be resolved between these two banks and the mechanisms that facilitated such payment requests if they acted as guarantors. The central bank may have nothing to do with it if it did not guarantee the availability of resources to back such a request. At the time of recalling and replacement, this central bank is only recalling the paper currency it had previously issued to keep the economy working efficiently and it is now replacing it with electronic currency. This central bank should never increase the money supply in order to resolve a dispute between banks as it will increase the amount of money issued by more than it initially supplied. So, when a central bank increases the supply of electronic currency to more than the paper currency that was already there it will result in unfavourable economic trends. Secondly, the investigations into why a bank requested another bank to pay more than it had may not deliver any results if central banks fulfil promises on behalf of banks, as it will not deter them from such behaviour in the future.

Recalling and replacement procedure – cont'd 5

The monetary policy of your central bank dictated it to maintain the volume of paper currency notes at a certain level, so it is only the paper currency notes that are recalled and replaced with electronic currency. The figures sitting inside your bank account have a value because they represent these currency notes, which are legal tender issued by your central bank.

Paper currency is issued by a central bank and used to settle ordinary day-to-day transactions. Anything except paper currency that may have been issued as legal tender, bond or a promise by a government or its agencies but is not used the way paper currency is used should not be replaced with electronic currency.

This transition is from a paper currency economy to a paper currency-free economy, and as such only paper currency should be recalled and replaced with electronic currency. If any other legal tenders, promises or bonds were issued by a central bank or a government that are transferable or can be used to settle debt, but are not used the way paper currency is used, then they should not be recalled and replaced with electronic currency. They exist in their own domain and as such they should not be replaced.

Such legal tenders, promises or bonds can continue to be used for the purposes for which they were issued or have been used, or they can be bought back by a central bank or government and the money transferred to the seller's account, but it should not be replaced with electronic currency because:

1. It is not used by entities the way they use paper currency.
2. Replacing it with electronic currency will result in increasing the supply of money within your economy from what it was when paper currency was present. If you replace that legal tender with electronic currency you are treating both as equal, whereas before

this they were not equal because paper currency had its own use and domain, which was that it was used by entities to buy and sell goods and services and was transferrable between any two entities without any formalities at any time, anywhere within a jurisdiction and has been used to satisfy any debt. If any other legal tender exists apart from the paper currency, then the two cannot be treated equally.

3. Replacing any legal tender other than the paper currency will have a negative impact on an economy. It will just be equal to printing new currency notes without the corresponding increase in production.

When special legal tenders are issued to settle transactions for special purposes then they are not paper currency and they operate in their own domain and for purposes for which paper currency is not used. If you replace these special legal tenders with electronic currency then they will enter the same domain as paper currency in the form of newly created electronic currency, and that electronic currency will be used to buy production. This will increase the supply of money so there will be more money and the same level of production, which will give rise to unfavourable economic trends.

If those special legal tenders were sold by a government, then they would have been sold after the buyer transferred money into a bank account nominated by a government. This legal tender or promise was sold for paper currency already in existence; that paper currency represented the production in existence, so when a government is buying it back, it has to buy it back with the currency already in existence.

Let's look at this illustration, where a government issued a special legal tender or a bond, which is a legal tender to satisfy a debt, and Entity A buys it. The balance sheet of this bank, where both have their accounts, looks like this before the transaction:

Table 3.63 Balance sheet before transaction

Balance Sheet Bank 1			
Cash	5,000	Government	3,000
		Entity A	2,000
Total	**5,000**	**Total**	**5,000**

The balance sheet after the transaction, where Entity A has bought the special purpose legal tender for 1,000 dollars, looks like this:

Table 3.64 Balance sheet after Entity A purchases special legal tender

Balance Sheet Bank 1			
Cash	5,000	Government	4,000
		Entity A	1,000
Total	**5,000**	**Total**	**5,000**

The overall position of cash within this economy has not changed. Now at the time of recalling and replacement, a government cannot convert both the paper currency and this other legal tender into electronic currency. Doing that will increase the supply of money to 6,000, which is 1,000 more than what was originally there. This will amount to printing extra money at a time when the level of production is the same, which will result in unfavourable economic trends in the economy.

Need for paper currency to settle international transactions

After transition to a paper currency-free economy, entities that travel to your country can:

- Transfer money electronically between bank accounts located in various jurisdictions
- Make payments with their debit or credit cards
- Exchange their traveller's cheques for your local electronic currency
- Exchange another foreign currency for your local electronic currency.

Entities that trade with your country can:

- Transfer money electronically between bank accounts located in various jurisdictions
- Use other instruments of banking to make payments and settle transactions.

Banks and certain other entities that facilitate the settlement of transactions at the international level are very much a part of this system.

Since the discussion is about the transition to a paper currency-free economy, a question can arise about how those international transactions would be settled where paper currency is used today or might need to be used, if at all, in the absence of a mechanism to settle transactions electronically or otherwise. How will the system work if paper currency is needed to settle transactions? You would have seen from the discussion above that paper currency will not be needed to settle transactions domestically as electronic currency accounts will provide the solution.

So, what if paper currency is needed to settle transactions at the international level? This part discusses that aspect of the transition to a paper currency-free economy. From the discussion so far we can see that that situation may arise to settle transactions between banks, governments and other entities that facilitate the settlement of financial transactions internationally.

Paper currency can exist to settle transactions if needed, but the use of your country's paper currency should be restricted to solely settling transactions between banks, governments and other entities that facilitate the settlement of transactions at the international level.

That paper currency may have all the characteristics of the paper currency in use today, such as a currency note number, a denomination, being a legal tender to settle a debt and issued by the central bank of your country, but with the following differences:

- The denomination should be higher for these currency notes, for example the notes should have a denomination of 1,000,000 units or above, measured against a currency used for trade at the international level. For example, if one unit of Currency X is equal to 100 units of Currency Y and Currency X is accepted internationally for the settlement of transactions then the smallest paper currency note of Currency Y kept to settle international transactions may have a denomination of 100,000,000. This is required for two reasons: firstly banks or governments or other specified entities will be settling only big transactions, and secondly a higher denomination will also mean that these currency notes will not fall into the hands of other entities.
- These currency notes should only be tradeable/exchangeable between governments, banks or other specified entities who should not be allowed to accept these currency notes from anyone except other banks, governments or specified entities. Possession by any other entity or acceptance from any other entity should be prohibited by law.

The following illustration explains this in detail:

Two banks operating in different jurisdictions need paper currency to settle their transactions. Let's say that Country A is a country where there is no paper currency in use. A person who has a savings account with a bank in Country A comes to Country B and spends 1,000 dollars using his debit card. For the purposes of this illustration let's assume that both currencies have the same value and that the balance sheet of the bank in Country A before that spending looks like this:

Table 3.65 Balance sheet of Bank A before electronic currency is exchanged for paper currency

Assets	Amount	Liabilities	Amount
Electronic Currency	2,000	Creditor	2,000

The 1,000 dollar debit card transaction has gone through electronically, but now to finally settle the transaction, the bank in Country A has to give 1,000 dollars (in paper currency) to the bank in Country B. The bank in Country A approaches the central bank of Country A and obtains 1,000 dollars in paper currency issued by the central bank of Country A in exchange for 1,000 dollars in electronic currency, and gives 1,000 dollars in paper currency to the bank in Country B. The balance sheet of this bank in Country A after that transaction will look like this:

Table 3.66 Balance sheet of Bank A after it has exchanged its electronic currency for paper currency

Assets	Amount	Liabilities	Amount
Electronic Currency	1,000	Creditor	1,000

The balance sheet of the bank in Country B will look like this after the transaction:

Table 3.67 Balance sheet of Bank B after it has received foreign paper currency

Assets	Amount	Liabilities	Amount
Foreign Paper Currency of Country A	1,000	Creditor	1,000

Which currency is used and which bank accounts are affected when entities settle their transactions?

The following questions will need to be answered and the solutions implemented by a central bank before transition to a paper currency-free economy.

The questions are:

1. When production of goods or services is generated within your economic jurisdiction or sold within your economic jurisdiction or imported from a foreign jurisdiction to your economic jurisdiction or exported from your economic jurisdiction to a foreign jurisdiction, which currency is used or which electronic currency accounts are affected and which bank accounts (the bank accounts present in banks situated within your economic jurisdiction or the bank accounts present in banks situated outside your economic jurisdiction) get affected to settle transactions, when entities party to the above mentioned generation, sale, import or export of production are:
   a. Natural or artificial
   b. Domestic or foreign
   c. Resident or non-resident for taxation purposes within your economic jurisdiction
   d. Physically present or not within your economic jurisdiction
   e. Present online only.
   Answering, and implementing the answers to, this question may ensure that:
   a. Your economy gets the full benefit of the production generated within it, from the point of production to the point when it is fully consumed or leaves your jurisdiction
   b. The production generated within your economic jurisdiction is fully represented in monetary terms in your currency.
2. When is it that only your local electronic currency is used to settle a transaction, and when is it that a foreign currency can be used?
3. When is it that only bank accounts present in banks operating from within your economic jurisdiction are affected, and when is it that bank accounts present in banks operating from outside your economic jurisdiction are used to settle a debt or a transaction?
4. When entities transfer money between bank accounts present in banks operating from within your economic jurisdiction for purposes other than the sale or purchase of goods and services, which electronic currency accounts are affected and which currency is used?

The effective implementation of the answers to these questions may determine:

1. How effectively a central bank controls the volume of money within its economic jurisdiction
2. How effectively a central bank implements its monetary policy
3. The value of your currency in relation to other currencies

4. The growth of your economy
5. The tax your tax authorities are entitled to.

The significance of these questions will increase as other central banks transition to electronic currency and banks present within your jurisdiction have electronic currency accounts issued by them.

These questions have to be answered by a central bank as it is a central bank that is responsible for achieving the results of its monetary policy and its impact within its economic jurisdiction.

By implementing the answers to these questions, a central bank will be able to influence the volume of money within its economic jurisdiction.

The above list of questions may be expanded to ensure that:

1. Your central bank's monetary policy determines the volume of currency in your economy
2. Your central bank is in control of the supply of money in your economy.

When a country transitions to a paper currency-free economy it is imperative that it explicitly bans the use of any paper currency from any part of the world to settle a transaction within its economic jurisdiction.

Let's look at this illustration to understand this. Entity 1 works for Entity 2 in Country 1. The production is generated within the economic jurisdiction of Country 1. Entity 2's products are sold in Country 1 and around the world.

Assume Entity 1 and Entity 2 to be one or more of the following at a time:

a. Natural or incorporated
b. Domestic or foreign
c. Resident or non-resident for taxation purposes within your economic jurisdiction
d. Physically present or not within your economic jurisdiction
e. Present online only.

and then answer the following questions:

1. In which currency and through which bank accounts should Entity 1 be paid so that:
    a. the GDP growth rate of your country is adequately reflected in your currency
    b. your tax authorities can get their due tax income?
2. In which currency and through which bank accounts should Entity 2's production be sold to entities (domestic and foreign) so that:

    a.   your GDP growth rate is adequately reflected in your currency
    b.   your tax authorities can get their due tax income
    c.   your central bank can determine the correct volume of currency needed for the effective functioning of your economy?

If the above questions are not answered, then in addition to what is mentioned under points 1 and 2 above, your central bank will not be able to regulate the volume of money supply within your economy, as banks will be free to transfer any currency or any electronic currency equivalent to the price in your currency to settle the transactions. When the above questions have been answered and the banks directed accordingly, the banks will have to use the currency determined by your central bank, which will be in a much better position to monitor and control the supply of money to achieve the objectives of its monetary policy.

Undirectional conversion needs oversight and direction

The discussion in this part deals with what happens when a foreign entity buys or consumes the goods and services available for consumption within your jurisdiction. The entity can either be artificial or natural. Let's assume that only your currency can be used to buy production within your jurisdiction. Foreign entities gain the ability to buy production which can be bought with your currency when their currency is converted into your currency. The impact of this is that:

1.   The foreign and domestic entities now have a foreign currency, which has been brought in by the foreign entity
2.   This foreign entity can use your currency to buy the products that can be bought with your currency
3.   The foreign currency brought in by the foreign entity can also be used to buy production generated outside your economic jurisdiction, so that the level of production available and the level of consumption of entities resident within your economic jurisdiction does not decline
4.   If foreign production is not bought with that foreign currency and the foreign entity consumes production present within your jurisdiction with your currency, then your domestic entities have sacrificed their production for no gain. The assumption here is that the goods and services consumed by the foreign entity within your jurisdiction are not in surplus.

Let's understand this with a simple illustration. There is a bank operating within your jurisdiction. This is its balance sheet.

Table 3.68 Balance sheet of a bank before a foreign entity deposits a foreign currency

Assets	Amount	Liabilities	Amount
Local Currency	100	Creditor 1	20
		Creditor 2	20
		Creditor 3	20
		Creditor 4	20
		Creditor 5	20

Now a foreign entity Creditor A brings 100 units of a foreign currency; the balance sheet of this bank will look like this:

Table 3.69 Balance sheet of a bank after a foreign entity has deposited foreign currency

Assets	Amount	Liabilities	Amount
Local Currency	100	Creditor 1	20
Foreign Currency	100	Creditor 2	20
		Creditor 3	20
		Creditor 4	20
		Creditor 5	20
		Creditor A	100

So, here the production available for consumption within your economic jurisdiction (assuming it is not surplus) and the local currency have remained the same as before, but the number of entities which can buy that production has increased. If production is not bought with foreign currency from outside your economic jurisdiction then the level of consumption of the entities present in your economic jurisdiction before Creditor A arrived with foreign currency may decline. So, to keep the level of consumption at the previous level, production must be bought with foreign currency brought in by Creditor A so that the amount of production available for consumption and consumption remain at the level they were before.

Domestically, Creditor A has five times more resources than any of the other five. So, despite being a foreign entity, it is able to spend more to buy the production available domestically. That production might have been generated by the other five, but because Creditor A has more resources, it can buy that production. So, the question is how do you ensure that your domestic entities do not have to sacrifice their consumption because of foreign entities who have more purchasing power? Not answering this question can lead to dissatisfaction among your domestic entities. Answering and implementing the answer to this question will also ensure that entities which launder money will not be able to invest the proceeds within your economy or to artificially create temporary booms within your economy. This question has probably never been answered at the depth required because governments feel happy that money is coming into their economies, without investigating what is happening with that money, how that money is getting used, who is buying production and who is losing out because someone else can pay more. An artificial temporary boom can only lead to recession or depression because consumption, which received an artificial boost, will eventually return to its normal pattern.

Let's delve a bit deeper. In the above illustration five domestic entities have twenty units of currency available and one foreign entity has 100 units of currency available to it, and within your economic jurisdiction only your currency can be used to settle transactions. So, the starting point here is that to buy production available for consumption domestically within your jurisdiction, Creditor A will not have access to more than twenty units of your local currency (to buy production outside your jurisdiction it is free to use all the foreign currency it has brought with it or other currencies as available). What this twenty unit local currency limit will do is create a level playing field between your domestic entities and the foreign entity, i.e. Creditor A. Now Creditor A will not be able to cause temporary booms within your economy and your domestic entities will not have to sacrifice their share of production available domestically just because Creditor A has more purchasing power. In real life, a level playing field can be created by ascertaining the average money in the hands of an average domestic entity and only making available that much of your currency to an average foreign entity for a period of time and then converting more for the next period of time per foreign entity. Foreign entities coming to your country can be put into various classes so that your average domestic entity is not at a disadvantage and you continue to attract foreign investment.

Now the next question is, is it in the interest of your economy to let money sit in a bank account? You can allow that money to boost consumption or investment in certain targeted sectors where you want to boost consumption or investment, but again the inputs used there should not reduce the production available for consumption domestically if production is not in surplus. Letting foreign entities buy production that is in short supply within your economy will not serve the interests of your domestic entities.

What stops you from asking someone who is bringing money into your jurisdiction to produce documents or tax returns to show that it is not dirty money? What stops you from directing your institutional investors to accept money from an investor only if that money has been declared in a tax return in the country where that money originated? When your neighbour is hungry, you are not safe and when your neighbour is not developed, you cannot sell to him or her what you can produce. Dirty money has caused pain and underdevelopment somewhere and your neighbour's underdevelopment will not let you realise your full potential.

Platforms for the electronic transfer of money

A transition to a paper currency-free economy will undoubtedly involve platforms that will enable the transfer of money from one bank account to another, just the way platforms facilitate the transfer of money today. Platforms that enable the transfer of money between buyers and sellers or between two or more bank accounts perform a vital function, but they are not banks. Only platforms that are authorised to operate as such by a government should be able to operate as platforms within that jurisdiction. Platforms can be regulated by directing banks to transfer money only via authorised platforms. Not regulating the conditions under which platforms operate may allow these platforms to affect a fundamental element of every economy, which is the availability of money.

What these platforms are allowed to do and what they cannot do will have to be specified and regulated. The following must be taken into consideration. The platforms should not be able to increase or decrease the volume of money in any way. Their work should be very simple, i.e. they facilitate the transfer of money between bank accounts. They do not increase or decrease the volume of money nor do they increase or decrease the availability of money in any way in any particular economic jurisdiction. They take money out of one bank account and deposit it in the destination bank account as fast as it is practical to do so. The question regarding which bank account is affected and which currency is used has been discussed above. When an entity transfers money to another entity's bank account via a platform, the platform takes money out of the transferring entity's bank account and immediately transfers it to the destination bank account . If it is charging the buying or selling entity a commission, then the platform can only transfer that commission to its own bank account.

If the platforms are able to increase or decrease the volume of money or its availability, then the central bank responsible for a jurisdiction will not be able to exercise its monetary policy the way it intends to and its control over the effective implementation of its monetary policy will be reduced.

Let's look at this illustration to understand the concept. Entity A transfers 1,000 dollars to Entity B electronically via a platform. The platform transfers only 500 dollars to Entity B's bank account and keeps the remaining 500 in its bank account. Those 500 dollars can be sitting within or outside your economy in one of the electronic currency accounts issued by your central bank. When a platform does not transfer the full amount and keeps it in its bank account, whether within your jurisdiction or outside, then the availability of money within the economy is reduced; the volume of money here has not changed but its availability has decreased. The entities now have 500 dollars less than before to continue their trade, which will have an impact on everything they do. This will start at the micro level, i.e. the level of an entity, and then be felt at the level of the whole economy, both domestic and global. Because firstly, this entity will have 500 dollars less and it will buy 500 dollars' worth less, and those who sell to this entity will lose 500 dollars in sales and this circle will go on, touching every entity within this economy because no entity within an economy is an island: everyone is connected to everyone else and the combined entities in this economy will have 500 dollars less when dealing with the rest of the world, so the rest of the world will also feel the impact. If this is not regulated from the beginning, some platforms might be able to increase or decrease the availability of money to the detriment of your economy and to their own advantage.

The requirements to operate as a platform must be stringent because:

a. They may have access to a lot of information
b. They may have the ability to take more money out of a bank account than intended by the account holder.

For purposes of online transfers of money, the platforms as a minimum must verify that the entity which is claiming to be lawful operator of a certain bank account does in fact control that account. The platform should not just take money out of a certain bank account or transfer money into a certain bank account merely on someone making the bank account details available. This verification must be a prerequisite before an entity can transfer or receive funds into a bank account using that platform. This verification is performed by some platforms presently.

How will criminals evade the system?

I find it very pertinent to discuss an example of how a corrupt or criminal entity might try to evade the system after the transition to a paper currency-free economy.

The question here is how will the sellers of contraband, the corrupt and other criminals who commit crime for money continue their business when you have transitioned to a paper currency-free economy?

The purpose of discussing this is to mention one of the ways they can use to avoid law enforcement and continue to give the pain they do. Law enforcement agencies, central banks and governments will have to keep their eyes open to see how criminals evade the system and devise ways to stop the crime that is committed for money. Please look at the flow chart below to see how criminals could continue their business.

In Figure 3.1, two entities want to do any or all of the following:

1. Buy or sell drugs
2. Buy or sell other contraband
3. Pay for or receive money for prostitution
4. Pay for or receive money for anything that is illegal within your jurisdiction
5. Launder money.

The paying entity might transfer 1,000 dollars and may not buy small quantities; the seller may deliver only after the payment has been credited to its foreign bank account. This can apply to every crime committed for money.

Now these entities do not want to transfer or receive money from or into their bank accounts held at banks that operate in your jurisdiction because that would be visible and your law enforcement agencies could investigate and take action against them.

The question then is: how will they move their money?

In the flow chart, Entity 1 transfers money from its bank account at a bank in your jurisdiction to its bank account in a foreign, most likely a secrecy jurisdiction, and then to the seller's bank account held at a bank in a foreign jurisdiction. So now the drugs were sold or any other illegal act was done in your jurisdiction but the payment was made in a foreign jurisdiction. That money will again travel back to your economic jurisdiction as most currencies are convertible. This process should not be considered a cumbersome process; in fact when you transition to a paper currency-free economy, such bank accounts and schemes to help criminals do what they have always done will be

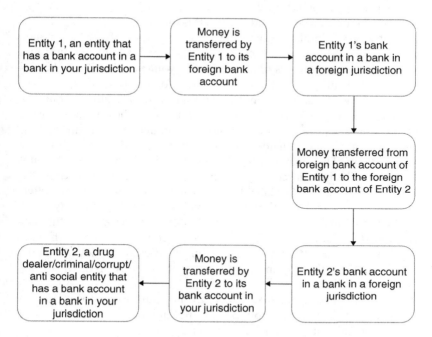

Figure 3.1 How entities may evade the system to continue their unlawful business

available in plenty – but only if you have not set your house in order and if you did not think ahead about how they were going to evade the system.

In the above flow chart, it will be visible to authorities in your part of the world as to which foreign bank money was transferred to and from which foreign bank money has been transferred to a bank account in your jurisdiction when the seller transfers money from its foreign bank to its bank account in your jurisdiction. But what will not be visible is that there was a transfer of money between two bank accounts in that foreign jurisdiction, and because of that transfer a criminal act was committed in your jurisdiction and the seller of that crime will be able to use the resulting money in your jurisdiction. Because most currencies are convertible it will not matter whether that foreign bank has an electronic currency account issued by your central bank. Even at a time when you have transitioned to electronic currency and banks in your jurisdiction use electronic currency accounts issued by your central bank, the present system of settlement of payments can continue.

The next question is how does this seller of drugs or contraband, corrupt official or a money launderer use this money?

That is very simple: he uses the debit or credit card validly issued by his bank and keeps transferring money from his bank account in a secrecy jurisdiction to his bank account in your jurisdiction, or he creates a facade entity if the scale of his operations is large.

Now, the next question is not is it easy to open a bank account at a bank in a secrecy jurisdiction? The question is, can these bank accounts be made available to the corrupt and the criminal in the future? These bank accounts could be made available online, especially if there is no law against them. They may not require any identification and the account holder may be recognised only by an account number and a password. Many banks might like to take this opportunity to make a profit by offering online bank accounts that do not require any proof of identity.

Such bank accounts may be made available very easily and the process could be made even simpler and faster at a time when all the corrupt and criminal entities present in your jurisdiction will want to find a way to continue their business. So, what is needed to stop this?

1.   A simple law that banks which are not authorised to operate as banks in your jurisdiction cannot offer any bank accounts in your jurisdiction either online or otherwise

2.   Banks that are authorised to operate as banks can offer bank accounts only when they have completed the formalities required by law regarding the identity of anyone who wants to hold a bank account with them

3.   It must be a criminal offence for entities that have a bank account in your jurisdiction to also have any bank accounts in any jurisdiction that does not require verification of the identity of the account holder or to have bank accounts where no identity is required

4.   It must be a criminal offence for any bank, which may operate as a bank in any part of the world, to offer a bank account either online or otherwise, to any entity in your jurisdiction if that bank is not authorised to operate as a bank in your jurisdiction

5.   Direct your banks and platforms to not transfer money to banks that are used by criminals, money launderers and antisocial elements to transfer money clandestinely (or if money is genuinely needed to be transferred to a bank account with those banks, the purpose must be verified and the documents audited before the transfer)

6.   Banks that are authorised to operate as banks in your jurisdiction will inform your government if they assist or have assisted, either

directly, as an advisor or in any other way, any entity that has a bank account with them in your jurisdiction to open a bank account in a foreign jurisdiction, form an entity outside your jurisdiction or to move money from your jurisdiction to a foreign jurisdiction or from a foreign jurisdiction to your jurisdiction. Banks will also inform your government if they have any relationship with anyone who presently does or has previously done any of the above for entities that have a bank account with them in your jurisdiction

7. Any other measures your law enforcement agencies, central bank or government deem necessary.

Central bank is in the centre

You would have noticed throughout this discussion that a lot of trust has been placed in central banks, which are agencies of governments. That is because under most circumstances, a central bank can be trusted more than a corporation, whose objective could be to maximise the wealth of its shareholders, or perhaps to maximise the wealth of its CEOs and directors; either way, they are not too concerned about maximising the welfare of the community. Governments work for the welfare of their people, or at least claim to, and governments do need a certain level of public support to exist, and that is why a little more trust, sceptically of course, can be placed in a central bank.

The choice rests with us

When in any community or country, there is a discussion on whether we should move towards a paper currency-free economy. A very important question that deserves discussion is what negative impact or harm will a transition to a paper currency-free economy have on your community and your country, and how can that negative impact or harm be mitigated?

We can continue to live the way we are or we can strive to make changes that will make our society a better place. The choice rests with us. The transition to a paper currency-free economy to one where the movement of money from one entity to another is visible will help stop corruption and professional crime, will give a boost to economic development and will empower us, the people who inhabit this Earth.

Index

Printed in the United States
by Baker & Taylor Publisher Services